DUAL DISASTERS

DUAL DISASTERS

Humanitarian Aid After the 2004 Tsunami

Jennifer Hyndman

Kumarian Press
An Imprint of Stylus Publishing

Dual Disasters: Humanitarian Aid After the 2004 Tsunami
Published in 2011 in the United States of America by Kumarian Press,
22883 Quicksilver Drive, Sterling, VA 20166 USA.

Design by Pro Production Graphic Services
Copyedit by Bob Land
Proofread by Sue Boshers
Index by Robert Swanson
The text of this book is set in 11/14 Adobe Garamond

Cover photo courtesy of DefenseImagery.mil. Use does not imply or constitute Department of Defense endorsement.

Printed in the USA on acid-free paper by IBT Global.

∞ The paper used in this publication meets the minimum requirements of the American National Standard for Information Sciences—Permanence of Paper for printed Library Materials, ANSI Z39.48–1984

Library of Congress Cataloging-in-Publication Data

Hyndman, Jennifer.
Dual disasters : humanitarian aid after the 2004 Tsunami / Jennifer Hyndman.
    p.   cm.
  Includes bibliographical references and index.
  ISBN 978-1-56549-335-3 (pbk. : alk. paper) — ISBN 978-1-56549-336-0
    (cloth : alk. paper) — ISBN 978-1-56549-382-7 (library ebook) —
    ISBN 978-1-56549-383-4 (consumer ebook)
  1. Indian Ocean Tsunami, 2004. 2. Tsunami relief—Indonesia—Aceh.
3. Tsunami relief—Sri Lanka. 4. Humanitarian assistance—Indonesia—Aceh.
5. Humanitarian assistance—Sri Lanka. 6. Aceh (Indonesia)—Social conditions.
7. Aceh (Indonesia)—Politics and government. 8. Sri Lanka—Social conditions.
9. Sri Lanka—Politics and government. I. Title.
  GC222.I45H96   2011
  363.34'9480959811—dc22
                                                            2010043185

This book is dedicated to all the people who lost their lives in Sri Lanka and Aceh due to decades of conflict and to the unprecedented waves of December 26, 2004, and to those who survived, showing unimaginable resilience and strength.

For Alison, who makes all things possible.

Contents

Illustrations

All photos in the book are by the author unless otherwise noted.

Figures

Tables

Preface

"The tsunami changes everything," said the new Canadian high commissioner to Sri Lanka in an interview early in 2005. In that moment, she was referring to Canada's decision to continue bilateral funding to Sri Lanka, even though Canada had been plotting its exit as a donor of international aid. Indeed, the 2004 tsunami changed everything, from environmental practices to gender relations to violent conflict. This book probes these developments and dynamics in Aceh, Indonesia, and Sri Lanka, where the waves hit hardest.

Monument to Those Who Died in the Tsunami

A disaster is a catastrophe that results in significant human and sometimes physical destruction due to violent conflict or environmental hazards. Such calamities can occur simultaneously in a single place, resulting in dual or even multiple disasters at once. Analyzing the impact of such crises and the new spaces and meanings created by them, I aim to shed light on the underbelly of globalization: the places where war and poverty intersect, where human displacement and environmental destruction are the flotsam and jetsam of a capricious global polity.

As I sit down to write this preface, humanitarian disasters of the past are remembered. The people of Srebrenica mark the fifteenth anniversary of the mass slaughter of men and boys who were their sons, husbands, friends, and neighbors. Six months have passed since the earthquake in Haiti, yet the media remind us that most of those affected remain in squalid housing conditions. The 2004 tsunami recalibrated loss on an unprecedented scale. Where in conflict, a family might lose a loved one, the tsunami wiped out entire families, sometimes leaving just one survivor.

Humanitarian crises affect people differently, of course, depending on their geographic, economic, and social locations. They precipitate change, increasing vulnerabilities on the one hand, but also opening up new possibilities on the other. And when disasters occur together, aid must be delivered in ways that are conflict-sensitive so that war is not unwittingly fueled by the impulse to help those in need.

This book is dedicated first and foremost to the people who survived the tsunami, and the conflicts, in Aceh and Sri Lanka. Their resilience has inspired me time and again during the years of research on which this book is based. While I do not know the pain and loss they have suffered, they have generously shared their stories, insights, and experiences of both war and the huge waves. By focusing on international responses to crises like the 2004 tsunami and the wars that preceded it in Sri Lanka and Aceh, my hope is that critical analysis of actions taken can make a difference in the lives of people displaced by disasters to come.

Acknowledgments

This book could not have been written without the collaboration of many people, to whom I express my deepest gratitude. I have been working with my friend and anthropological colleague, Mala de Alwis, for more than a decade on various projects in Sri Lanka, including this one. In 2006 I met Arno Waizenegger in Vancouver, where he was an exchange student conducting research in Aceh funded by the Asia-Pacific Foundation. Philippe Le Billon introduced me to Arno, a serendipitous moment for which I am thoroughly grateful. Arno and I began three seasons of fieldwork in Aceh in June 2007, resulting in a pair of films, a forthcoming chapter, and much of what appears in Chapter 6. Thank you, Arno.

So many other minds, hands, and tongues assisted with this work. Thanks to Lisa Brunner and Natalie Crook, who were at the forefront of editing earlier drafts of the chapters and giving bibliographic help when needed. Soundarie David provided vital research assistance in Colombo in 2007 for a segment of this project funded by Canada International Development Research Centre. I appreciate the contributions of both Soundarie and IDRC.

Tim Bunnell, Lotta Hedman, Saiful Madhi, Vani Simon, Vijay Kumar, Kumari Jayawardena, Sunil Bastian, Alice Nah, Dan Hiebert, Wenona Giles, and Peter Meekison all contributed expert advice at various points throughout the research. A number of graduate students also participated in the research: Arif Jamal, Sarah Paynter, Kathy Sherrell, Rini Sumartojo, Jessi Lehman, Robert Lidstone, and James McLean.

John Ng offered his cartographic skills featured in the pages that follow, and Liliana Hill made paying for the research possible. Thanks to you all.

I am grateful for the support of the Social Sciences and Humanities Research Council of Canada (SSHRC) that funded the lion's share of this research through its standard grant program.

Finally, inspiration and support from home made this all possible. Ali, you are by far the best editor and writer in the family. Thank you, for everything.

I would like to thank Erica Flock and Jim Lance, both editors at Kumarian Press, for their work on the manuscript, from beginning to end. Their insights and persistent calls to fill in the blanks have made this a better book.

Publishers have kindly granted their permission to use segments from earlier work:

Hyndman, J. 2009. Same tsunami, different contexts: Siting conflict and peace in Sri Lanka and Aceh, Indonesia. *Norwegian Journal of Geography* 63(1): 89–96. Reproduced with permission from the publisher (Taylor & Francis Ltd., http://www.informaworld.com).

Hyndman, J. 2007. The securitization of fear in post-tsunami Sri Lanka. *Annals of the Association of American Geographer,* 97(2): 361–72. Copyright is held by the AAG, and journal details are available at http://www.informaworld.com.

Hyndman, J. 2008. Feminism, conflict and disasters in post-tsunami Sri Lanka. Originally published in *Gender Technology and Development* 12(1): 101–21. Copyright © Gender and Development Studies Center, Asian Institute of Technology, Thailand. All rights reserved. Reproduced with the permission of the copyright holders and the publishers, Sage Publications India Pvt. Ltd., New Delhi.

Hyndman, J. 2009. Acts of aid: Neoliberalism in a war zone. *Antipode* 41(5): 867–89. Reproduced with the permission of the copyright holders and the publishers, John Wiley and Sons Inc.

Waizenegger, A., and J. Hyndman. 2010. Two solitudes: Post-tsunami and post-conflict Aceh. *Disasters* 34(3): 787–808. Reproduced with the permission of the copyright holders and the publishers, John Wiley and Sons Inc.

Abbreviations

AIC	Advanced industrial countries
AIDS	Acquired Immune Deficiency Syndrome
ALNAP	Active Learning Network for Accountability and Performance in Humanitarian Action
AMM	Aceh Monitoring Mission
ANRHR	Alliance for Protection of National Resources and Human Rights
ASEAN	Association of Southeast Asian Nations
ASNLF	Aceh/Sumatra National Liberation Front
BRA	*Badan Reintegrasi Damai Aceh* (Aceh Peace-Reintegration Agency)
BRR	*Badan Rehabilitasi dan Rekonstruksi* (Rehabilitation and Reconstruction Agency for Aceh and Nias)
CAD	Canadian dollar
CARE	Originally Cooperative for American Remittances to Europe, now Cooperative for Assistance and Relief Everywhere
CBC	Canadian Broadcasting Corporation
CFA	Ceasefire agreement
CIA	Central Intelligence Agency
CIDA	Canadian International Development Agency
CMI	Crisis Management Initiative
CoHA	Cessation of Hostilities Agreement
DC	Developing country

DFID	Department for International Development
DNA	Deoxyribonucleic acid
DOM	*Daerah Operasi Militer* (Military Operations Zone)
EU	European Union
FAD	Feminism and development
FMIA	*Front Mujahidin Islam Aceh*
GAD	Gender and development
GAM	*Gerakan Aceh Merdeka* (Free Aceh Movement)
GoI	Government of Indonesia
GoSL	Government of Sri Lanka
GSP	Generalized System of Preferences
HDC	Henry Dunant Centre
HD Centre	Centre for Humanitarian Dialogue
HIC	Humanitarian Information Centre
HIV	Human Immunodeficiency Virus
HRW	Human Rights Watch
ICES	International Centre for Ethnic Studies
ICG	International Crisis Group
ICRC	International Committee of the Red Cross
IDP	Internally displaced person
IDR	Indonesian rupiah
IDRC	International Development Research Centre
IFI	International financial institution
IMF	International Monetary Fund
INGO	International nongovernmental organization
IRB	Immigration and Refugee Board
JHU	*Jathika Hela Urumaya* (National Heritage Party)
JVP	*Janatha Vimukthi Peramuna* (People's Liberation Front)
KPA	*Komite Peralihan Aceh* (Aceh Transition Committee)
LTTE	Liberation Tigers of Tamil Eelam
MONLAR	Movement for National Land and Agricultural Reform
MoU	Memorandum of Understanding
MP	Member of Parliament
MSF	*Médecins Sans Frontières* (Doctors Without Borders)
NAM	Non-Aligned Movement
NGHA	Nongovernmental humanitarian agency
NGO	Nongovernmental organization

OCHA	Office for the Coordination of Humanitarian Affairs
ODA	Official development assistance
OECD	Organization for the Economic Cooperation and Development
PA	Partai Aceh
PRSPs	Poverty Reduction Strategy Papers
P-TOMS	Post-Tsunami Operational Management Structure
RADA	Reconstruction and Development Agency
RIA	*Republik Islam Aceh*
SIRA	*Sentral Informasi Referendum Aceh* (Centre for an Aceh Referendum)
SIRA	*Suara Independen Rakyat* (The Independent Voice of the Acehnese People)
SLMM	Sri Lanka Monitoring Mission
SPDC	State Peace and Development Council
SSHRC	Social Sciences and Humanities Council of Canada
TAFREN	Task Force to Rebuild the Nation
TDZ	Tsunami disaster zone
TEC	Tsunami Evaluation Coalition
TNA	*Tentara Nasional Aceh* (National Army of Aceh)
TNI	*Tentara Nasional Indonesia* (Indonesian Military Forces)
TRO	Tamil Rehabilitation Organization
UN	United Nations
UNF	United National Front
UNHCR	United Nations High Commissioner for Refugees
UNICEF	United Nations Children's Emergency Fund
US	United States
UTHR(J)	University Teachers for Human Rights (Jaffna)
WAD	Women and development
WID	Women in development
WUSC	World University Service of Canada

1

Introducing Dual Disasters

The 2010 earthquake in Haiti devastated an already shaken country. The disaster underscored the extent to which preexisting vulnerabilities conditioned its impact. While the exact death toll remains unknown, an estimated 230,000 people have perished, roughly the same number who died in the 2004 Indian Ocean Basin tsunami. Beyond the fatality count, what do these crises have in common? Both affected countries with histories of political conflict, instability, and human displacement prior to the catastrophes. United Nations (UN) agencies and international nongovernmental organizations (INGOs) were already on the ground in Haiti, where hundreds of employees were staffing the UN mission, at the time the earthquake hit. The UN chief in Haiti, Hédi Annabi; his Brazilian deputy; and the Canadian police chief in charge of training officers in Haiti were all among the casualties of the quake.

This book examines how environmental disasters interact with political crises that precede them. Central to this task is the concept of dual disasters, where a humanitarian crisis with human-made political roots overlaps with a humanitarian crisis induced by environmental disaster. While this introduction outlines a global context for dual disasters, I primarily focus on the case of the 2004 tsunami and its impact in Aceh, Indonesia, and in Sri Lanka, where decades of civil war preceded the death and destruction of the waves in each. In Aceh, the crisis of the tsunami created diplomatic space for discussion and hastened a peace process. In Sri Lanka, responses to the disaster exacerbated tensions among Tamils, Muslims, and the Sinhala-dominated government.

1

Like Haiti at the time of the earthquake, Sri Lanka at the time of the tsunami hosted the UN Children's Emergency Fund (UNICEF), the UN High Commissioner for Refugees (UNHCR), the International Federation of the Red Cross (ICRC), and dozens of international NGOs that addressed conditions created by a civil war in that country. Because the tsunami wreaked havoc on the eastern and southern coasts but not in the capital, Colombo, the headquarters of the government and aid industry were largely unaffected, in contrast to Haiti's capital, Port-au-Prince. Nonetheless, the Haitian earthquake and Indian Ocean Basin tsunami overlaid contested political landscapes of conflict and dispossession that were in place well before these environmental disasters hit.

The adverse effects of the earthquake on the Haitian people are acute, but they cannot be separated from the existing landscape of its colonial history with France, its imperial occupations by the United States, the rise of authoritarian government throughout much of the twentieth century, and the political coups that have characterized the past twenty years of rule in Haiti. These political relationships of conflict at many levels produced the poverty in Haiti before the January 12, 2010, quake. Multiple crises may occur at once. Haiti is defined as much by preexisting layers of political instability and economic privation as by the earthquake that has now shattered the nation.

As I write this introduction, the drama of the rescue missions for those trapped under fallen buildings in Haiti has come to an end. Although most survivors are found within three days of such disasters, many defied the odds. One teenager was pulled alive from the rubble fifteen days after the earthquake; another emaciated man was found almost a month after the quake. While such events are reported and celebrated around the world through globalized media, the long-term benefits of relief efforts are not without controversy. More than $1 billion in emergency aid was pledged by governments and private individuals within days of the disaster, and much more was pledged at donor conferences in Montreal and New York early in 2010. Yet the question remains whether Haiti will simply be "built back better"—a common refrain among housing and reconstruction experts—or whether the future of the country depends on more than new schools, hospitals, roads, government buildings, economic advice, and loans. Caribbean historian Melanie Newton (2010) comments that "reconstruction efforts must aim at eliminating Haiti's terrible reality of *la misère,* the Haitian Kréyol word for the abject poverty that dominates the lives of most Haitians. As long as Haiti remains one of the world's most socio-economically un-equal countries, reconstruction efforts in Haiti are likely to re-create the structures exacerbating the current catastrophe." Instead of building back better, an approach that risks re-creating disparities that existed before the earthquake, experts have called for a new strategy.

In March 2010 at the New York donors' conference, the Interim Haitian Reconstruction Commission, chaired jointly by Haitian prime minister Jean-Max Bellerive and former US president Bill Clinton was established. The commission has the authority to seek, approve, and co-ordinate projects. The plan has yet to be approved by the Haitian people, though it seems to mitigate mistrust of both corrupt government and im-perial humanitarians that constitute the international community.

Disasters do not occur in a political or economic vacuum. Local ge-ographies of inequality, poverty, gender relations, ethnicity, and social and economic marginalization shape response and recovery for those who survive them (Sidaway et al. 2008). Yet international responses will also bear the imprint of geopolitical designs and strategic considerations (McGregor 2010).

There Is Simply No Such Thing as a Purely "Natural" Disaster

A brief examination of recent "environmental" disasters reveals the role of human factors. The earthquake in Gujarat in January 2001 was even stronger than the one measured in Haiti, if less deadly, killing over 20,000 people and injuring some 167,000. Patterns of discrimination in the reconstruction initiatives that followed related to broader patterns of extant social polarization (Simpson 2008).

On December 26, 2004, a tsunami captivated the world's attention; the huge waves washed away family members, homes, and hotels in the dramatic devastation. While Aceh was the hardest hit and closest to the epicenter of the shock that created the tsunami, the plight of people there received far less attention because foreigners were not allowed into the province. Unlike Thailand, a tourist mecca during holiday season, the destruction and loss experienced in Aceh came much later from local news media and people's cell phone footage (see Figure 1.1).

In the Maldives, far fewer died—only 108 people perished in the tsunami—but the estimate of damage and loss was nearly 80% of a year's gross national income (Cosgrave 2007). Because the site represented an almost exclusively coastal tourist economy, a great deal of infrastructure was destroyed. The human impact of the tsunami also varied dramatically across space, based on proximity to the epicenter, population density, and quality of housing structures: in Aceh the ratio of dead to injured was 6:1, falling to 1.5:1 in Sri Lanka (Cosgrave 2007).

The destruction of Hurricane Katrina—a First World disaster—followed the tsunami in August 2005. While the number of those who died was much lower than those of the other crises, the cost of reconstruction was by far the greatest. Commentators asked how such human calamity could be created in the world's remaining superpower. Some called the survivors of Katrina "refugees" because of the US government's inability to protect its citizens, both before the levees broke and after the hurricane hit. Others protested the "refugee" label, stating that its racialized

Figure 1.1 A Power-Generating Barge Transported Several Kilometers Inland by the Tsunami in Banda Aceh

connotations conjured an orientalist image of displaced people from places in Africa inappropriate for American citizens.

Later that year, in October 2005, the Pakistan earthquake in the Kashmir hit, but did not get the same attention as the tsunami or Hurricane Katrina, despite the death of almost 80,000 people and the displacement of millions more. The uneven global media coverage and world attention that these environmental disasters generate is a vital factor shaping international responses to crisis. Post-colonial ties, Cold War allegiances, and diasporic influence also help shape international responses to humanitarian disasters, whether they are human-made or tectonically derived.

Disasters are, then, not simply natural. Building codes, zoning policies, environmental regulations, and their enforcement (or not) shape the outcomes of major weather events, earthquakes, and tsunamis. Human vulnerability to these calamities and resilience in the face of them are conditioned by human factors, a commonsensical point but one that is often lost in the shuffle during humanitarian responses. Presentism is the idea that history is written through the logic and knowledge of the present, and that historical narrative does not depict the past in context on its own terms, but instead views it through one's current societal value system. Presentism is very much at work in places like Haiti.

Death and destruction in Haiti have been attributed to shoddy construction and inappropriate architectural designs built to withstand hurricanes rather than earthquakes. The collapsing concrete meant to withstand hurricane force winds has proven deadly, yet the observation that concrete could be a fatal building material if an earthquake hit did not emerge until after the quake. An impoverished state with limited building resources is blamed for having decimated a precious national resource: its schools (Revkin 2010):

> Early each morning, legions of children in crisp uniforms marched through the city's trash-strewn streets to study mathematics, civics, science and a variety of languages, a sign of hope that endured through coups, foreign interventions and natural disasters. (Booth and Wilson 2010)

The stubborn persistence of normalcy amid intermittent crises is impressive, but education officials estimate that the quake demolished thousands of schools, some 75% of those in the capital, Port-au-Prince, alone. An inventory is under way to determine the loss of teachers and staff. "Without education, we have nothing," said Michel Renau, director of national exams at the Ministry of National Education, Youth and Sports in Haiti, which itself is a pile of rubble in the city center. "We've been set back very far. But if we pull ourselves together quickly, we'll go on" (cited in Booth and Wilson 2010).

International aid to Haiti in the aftermath of the earthquake will rebuild schools and hospitals, as well as infrastructure. But can aid actors avoid presentist readings of the damage and devastation? Haiti's own historical geography—layers of violence, debt, and political coups—creates a context for understanding the current crisis in critical ways.

Haiti's Political Landscapes of Disaster

What happened to Haiti before the earthquake hit?

Haitians led the first successful slave revolt in modern history, and declared Haiti the first independent black republic in 1804. Haiti also became the second independent nation in the Western Hemisphere (Danner 2010). Analyzed from today's perspective, these political events are seen as unmitigated accomplishments, yet independence for Haitians was not easy in historical context. At the time, Haiti's emancipation was an affront to prevailing colonial powers where slavery continued. After declaring independence, Haitians burned the sugar plantations where they had been enslaved. France, the former colonial master, burdened Haiti in 1825 with massive reparation payments for property that included lost slaves and the plantations (Ward 2010a; Faul 2010). Meanwhile, the US government, concerned that Haiti's newfound independence might rub off on its own slave population, did not recognize Haiti for almost six decades.

The United States, along with major colonial powers of the time, imposed a trade embargo against Haiti, crippling its fledgling economy and forcing payment of the debt set by France: 150 million francs, a sum later lowered to 90 million (Faul 2010). In this post-colonial context of imperial design, Haiti's distorted political landscape emerged (Farmer 1994). In 1915 US marines occupied Haiti to enforce debt repayment and put an end to a violent struggle for power that was seen to threaten US interests. They stayed until 1934, and "laid part of the groundwork for the current disaster" (Newton 2010). No wonder "Haiti has had thirty coups and twenty constitutions" since its independence in 1804, according to Robert Muggah (cited in Ward 2010c).

Renewed antipathy against white foreign rulers culminated in 1957 with the rise of François Duvalier, also known as "Papa Doc," who ruled as dictator by force and by fear. He also managed to curry favor with the United States by using Cold War threats of communism to gain support abroad. Papa Doc's son and political heir, Jean-Claude (Baby Doc), ruled the country from 1971 until 1986, when he was overthrown.

In 1991 Haitians elected their own president, Jean-Bertrand Aristide, a priest from Haiti's slums who advocated higher wages for Haitians (Ward 2010a). He was removed from office in a Central Intelligence Agency (CIA)-backed coup that same year. Aristide regained power in 1994 and was reelected as president in 2000, before being toppled again in a violent 2004 coup (Dixon 2010). The current president, René Préval, is seen by critics as a representative of French, US, and Canadian interests.

This thumbnail sketch of recent political history is partial—both incomplete and critical of the colonial and imperial consequences that the Haitian people have disproportionately borne. Nonetheless, it aims to depict a country that is more than a rogue state, that is to say, a country unable or unwilling to steer its own course and plan its own future, a "basket case" in the words of one political commentator.[1] As this book aims to demonstrate, such representations of aid recipients are part and parcel of the geopolitical project of the international aid regime. Aid commands particular performances in exchange for the assistance given.

When the earthquake hit in January 2010, 40% of Haiti's annual budget was provided through international aid. By some estimates, there are 10,000 NGOs operating in Haiti (*Economist* 2010b), though only 550 are registered with the government.

The Politics of International Aid

Newton (2010) explains that "one of the most destabilizing aspects of Haiti's political history has been the use of aid and loans by powerful external donors in order to call the political shots, control Haiti's economy and facilitate the exploitation of its people." International aid is a geopolitical tool that donor states use to influence beneficiary governments and their people, as well as a basket of well-intentioned gifts and practical responses to human need and disaster. In the past decade Haiti has had $5 billion in international assistance (Ward 2010b).

Another aim of this book, then, is to show how aid policy influences people and their governments in areas affected by more than one kind of humanitarian disaster. The strings attached to international assistance shape its outcomes and efficacy. As Mark Danner (2010) explains, "Under the Duvaliers Haiti became the great petri dish of foreign aid." Aid tends to be granted on terms not of the recipient country's own making.[2]

Foreign assistance comes entangled with foreign ambitions, however altruistic its stated aims. Reconstruction in Haiti will cost billions of dollars, but how this aid is provided counts more than the amount or technical aspects of architecture and construction.

> This is not the first time that events in Haiti have served as harbingers for the world's collective future. An anti-slavery and anti-colonial revolution of 1791–1804 created the independent state of Haiti as only the second independent country in the Americas. In giving birth to Haiti, the revolution transformed the sociopolitical landscape of the 19th-century Atlantic world, unleashing forces that would ultimately lead to the collapse of Atlantic slavery. In a repeat of history, the 2010 earthquake has the potential to transform politics in our own times, either for better, or—if we fail to take the time to reflect deeply on the full meaning of what has happened—for worse. (Newton 2010)

Mark Schneider, senior vice president at the International Crisis Group, puts it this way: "It's not about building back better—but building with a vision created by Haitians" (cited in Diebel 2010). In a similar vein, Paul Farmer, who was former deputy UN special envoy to Haiti under President Clinton and a medical professor and doctor in rural Haiti for more than a decade, wrote in his book, *The Uses of Haiti* (1994, 374), "The first order of business, for citizens of the United States, might be a candid and careful assessment of our ruinous policies towards Haiti. . . . The Haitian people are asking not for charity, but for justice." He echoed this sentiment early in 2010 when he visited post-earthquake Haiti with former President Clinton.

Such an approach may, however, be more easily proposed than accomplished. The weak political leadership of a shaken president, René Préval, has not inspired confidence (Ward 2010c; Faul 2010). One of the historical consequences of political authoritarianism, instability, and corruption has been the exodus of many Haitians to new homes abroad. The loss of professionals, artists, and other aspiring citizens amounts to a serious brain drain for Haiti that represents a major challenge in the current crisis.

Members of the diaspora who left Haiti during earlier rounds of political crisis have joined forces with powerful Haitians living in the country to create a Marshall Plan of sorts to build a new Haiti. In February 2010, thirty-three Haitians drafted the Strategic Plan for National Salvation. This road map of 173 pages was thought to be the first comprehensive long-term national plan since the end of the Duvalier dictatorship in 1986 (Chung 2010). The plan's cost is estimated at $100 billion over twenty-five years. The fate of such a plan is unclear, and its relation to the proposed Interim Haitian Reconstruction Commission as yet unspecified, yet its authors have joined forces across geography to make a start, one that emphasizes autonomy as much as prosperity.

Addressing hard questions about who sets project priorities, governs aid distribution, and manages reconstruction in the highly charged context of Haiti is vital. After the 2004 tsunami in Aceh, Indonesia, the government was criticized for taking months to develop a plan for rehabilitation and reconstruction. This effectively left international humanitarian organizations to stabilize the crisis in the early weeks and months. Yet, a blueprint finally issued by the government of Indonesia (GoI) provided a detailed outline of what it wanted, asserting its sovereignty over the recovery process and over international aid agencies based in Aceh, a long contested region of its territory that had been closed to foreigners until the disaster hit.

Unlike Haiti, Indonesia's central government was in a position of stability and strength when the tsunami hit. While it has long fought insurgents in West Papua and in what is now the independent state of East Timor, as well as in Aceh, the government of Indonesia took charge of the reconstruction process after the tsunami. In contrast, the Haitian government had no roof under which to meet to discuss its work in the first months after the earthquake, let alone the resources or capacity to design and implement a blueprint such as the Strategic Plan for National Salvation mentioned above.

Learning From Disaster: If/Then

"Disaster is a disruption and unraveling of spatial or geographic order," Kenneth Hewitt contends (cited in Clark 2007, 1132). Disasters are difficult to study because they are multidimensional and processual, affecting all aspects of human life as well as the environment (Choi 2009). The idea that a disaster is not simply natural should be clear by now. A short overview of recent environmental disasters nonetheless serves to show exactly how this is so. In 2004 an earthquake off the tip of Sumatra Island, Indonesia, generated a momentous tsunami in the Indian Ocean Basin, affecting some twenty countries. Had these events occurred in the South Pacific where tsunamis are quite common, early warning systems would have been in place, notifying people of impending waves and saving lives. If the countries affected by the 2004 tsunami were more affluent, they might also have afforded these preventative measures before the tsunami hit, and outcomes could have been much different. Given government restrictions on access to Aceh for foreigners, images from that region took longer to emerge.

Less than a year after the 2004 tsunami, a major earthquake leveled homes in the contested Kashmir border region of Pakistan and, to a lesser extent, India, rendering 3.3 million survivors homeless (MacKinnon 2010). International public attention to and funds for the earthquake were significantly less than those for the tsunami, raising important questions of which "optics" foster giving from charitable strangers who witness such disasters from afar (Jeganathan 2005). The media coverage and visibility of the earthquake in remote Kashmir were far less than that for the tsunami in Thailand and Sri Lanka where foreign tourists videotaped the event.

Eight months later, in August 2005, Hurricane Katrina formed over the Bahamas, gained strength, and struck the US coasts of Florida, Louisiana, and Mississippi. Despite expert knowledge that the levees protecting New Orleans needed $15 billion worth of serious repairs to make the city safe, they were never funded. Instead the levees failed, and much of New Orleans was flooded. Safety was disparately apportioned:

those too infirm or poor to evacuate stayed put; those who could leave did. The confluence of racialized poverty, differentiated mobility, bad policy decisions (i.e., not to fund levee reconstruction), and global warming created an immense humanitarian disaster.

Hurricane Katrina was a moderate Category 1 hurricane when it hit southern Florida, but after gathering warmer water, wind, and force from the Gulf of Mexico, it struck the Louisiana coast as a lethal Category 3 or 4 hurricane (Gore 2006). Evidence shows that hurricanes are getting stronger due to global warming (Geist et al. 2006; Lovgren 2006). This means that dual, or multiple, disasters are likely to increase in the future, assuming current rates of global warming and conflict duration.

When Cyclone Nargis hit Burma (known as Myanmar in official parlance) in May 2008, 130,000 people along the Irrawaddy Delta were killed and over 2 million people displaced (McGregor 2010). This violent storm became a full-blown humanitarian disaster in part *because* of government policy. The military government or junta, known ironically as the State Peace and Development Council (SPDC), has ruled with impunity since 1990 when it ignored the outcome of elections. The subsequent regime has had scant regard for human life, let alone human rights. It permitted very little coverage of the cyclone's destruction to be seen in the international media, and virtually no international aid or staff was allowed into the area to assist those affected until almost one month after the cyclone hit. The idea that disaster is conditioned by existing policies and practices challenges the naturalness of a so-called natural disaster.

After Cyclone Nargis, not only was precious little information about the impact of the cyclone on the people of Burma made available but access to the affected areas was highly restricted for international researchers. Likewise, the governments of Thailand and India exerted their own sovereignty and status as regional superpowers after the tsunami, declining much of the financial aid offered by international governments and opting instead to handle the crisis themselves. This decision is consistent with their policies and practices of development aid. Sovereignty is not just a consideration in contexts of conflict, territory, and insecurity, but also shapes humanitarian landscapes of dual disasters in profound ways.

On May 12, 2008, a massive earthquake of magnitude 7.9 hit Sichuan Province, China. Some 90,000 people were killed, among them 19,000 children who were crushed in poorly built school buildings that collapsed at the time of the quake (MacKinnon 2010). Since 1976, when the Tangshan earthquake in China killed over 240,000 people, the government has required that new structures be built to withstand major quakes. Yet the collapse of schools, hospitals, and factories in several different areas around Sichuan raised serious questions about whether such codes were enforced during China's recent building boom (*New York Times* 2009). The alleged corruption of Chinese government officials, accused of ordering the construction of inferior public school buildings in order to skim funds for themselves, created public outrage.

At least three officials committed suicide as the parents of deceased children signed petitions sent to the Central People's Party Government.[3] While most private schools remained standing after the quake, the public ones did not, highlighting the intersection of socioeconomic class differences in relation to survival. Moreover, China's one-child policy exacerbated the loss of these even more precious children for parents who had abided by the one-child edict. The human corruption of these policies played a huge part in terms of how and whom the disaster hit.

An earthquake of magnitude 8.8 rocked Chile in February 2010, prompting warnings in fifty-three countries ringing the Pacific Ocean, yet fatalities were in the hundreds, rather than the hundreds of thousands. Chile is a much wealthier country than Haiti. "On a per-capita basis, Chile has more world-renowned seismologists and earthquake engineers than anywhere else," states Brian Tucker of GeoHazards International (cited in Bajak 2010).

Chile possesses a robust emergency response capacity as well as a long history of managing seismic disasters. "Earthquakes don't kill—they don't create damage—if there's nothing to damage," according to Eric Calais, a Purdue University geophysicist (cited in Bajak 2010). The country has earthquakes regularly, and the country was prepared for this one. In 1960, after Chile's worst earthquake of magnitude 9.5, 1,655 people were killed and some 2 million left homeless. Haiti's last earthquake was 250 years ago, so readiness and a lack of resources to create capacity were both issues in that context.

Catastrophe as Opportunity?

Human displacement, due to conflict or a tsunami, is tied to other social, cultural, and economic displacements: the loss of existing authority structures, livelihoods, and local, quotidian routines. Often such losses increase people's vulnerability to hunger, violence, and homelessness.

> Struggles over interethnic justice, neo-liberalism, economic distribution, the disempowerment of women, caste bigotry and such have shaped the [Sri] Lankan political landscape in significant ways over the last decades. . . . Even the tsunami cannot wipe out the imprint of these fault lines. (Nesiah, Nanthikesan, and Kadirgamar 2005)

Fault lines result from human as well as geophysical forces, yet they can also open up space for other, more positive changes. Geographer Jim Glassman echoes this point with reference to Aceh:

> Many of the population have lived in conditions of poverty or near poverty throughout the years of the economic boom. Those who lived in small coastal villages eking out a living from the sea were among these, and their susceptibilities to an event like the tsunami are part and parcel of this poverty. (Glassman 2005, 165–66)

During the war between government troops and the Liberation Tigers of Tamil Eelam (LTTE) in Sri Lanka, government embargoes prevented basic staples like diesel fuel from getting into LTTE-held territory in the north. Accordingly, mobility became more restricted for those who had relied on public transportation. Women's travel to local food markets in rural areas was severely impeded due to a lack of available public bus service and to a cultural context that frowned upon married women riding bicycles, yet women slowly took up the two-wheeled option. Their mobility and autonomy increased, albeit in a context of conflict, scarcity, and necessity. Gender relations were destabilized by the war and remade in the context of the conflict. In Chapter 4, I show how the 2004 tsunami's destruction also remade social relations in unexpected ways.

Humanitarian disasters can unwittingly invoke social change. They can also create opportunities of a different sort. In her book *The Shock Doctrine*, Naomi Klein (2007) documents the opportunistic culture of "disaster capitalism" in the wake of calamity. She contends that disasters divert attention away from policy changes that often privatize public-sector services. Reconstruction can be big business for foreign lenders and contractors who are selected to do the necessary work. Disasters may also open up previously protected land to foreign investment and literally *capitalize* on havoc wreaked by disaster. Foreign companies can profit on the backs of disaster survivors.

One must be careful, however, to substantiate these claims empirically, and not overstate the deleterious impact of any one force. Klein convincingly shows her readers how specific US companies benefit from sizeable contracts to supply US troops in Iraq, but other claims are less scrupulously documented. She relies heavily on the evils of roaming global capitalism as an explanatory factor at the expense of competing nationalisms, historical legacies of colonialism, and prevailing geopolitics.

In Sri Lanka, for example, Klein (2007) visits the sleepy village of Arugam Bay on the hard-hit southeast coast in 2005. Known as a famous surfing beach with a handful of modest hotels for the budget traveler, Klein predicts an invasion of elite foreign hotels that would effectively privatize the beach and displace local fishers who have made their livelihoods there for generations. While this could still happen, I visited Arugam Bay in 2009 and stayed at the Stardust Hotel, in one of the higher-end rooms available, for about US$50. No boutique hotels or high-rise towers existed or were under construction, at least not in plain sight, as Klein had predicted. And yet new roads and land speculation for tourist sites were certainly features of the post-tsunami landscape.

Klein's analysis underestimates local and national actors in Sri Lanka that aspire to different futures. Her analysis denies much agency to the activist civil society organizations, elected officials, and unelected politicos that shape Sri Lankan society as much as the International Monetary Fund or Asian Development Bank.

China has offered to finance a new seaport and airport in Hambantota, the political seat of Sri Lankan president Mahinda Rajapakse, through soft loans of $1 billion. This stands as potential evidence for Klein's thesis. Yet the strategic location of Sri Lanka in the Indian Ocean also makes such assistance geopolitically savvy for China and for the president, who won the presidency handsomely again in January 2010. Access to a port here would be convenient for Chinese naval ships sent to guard the Indian Ocean sea lanes (*Economist* 2010a). Such investments are not solely based on economic gain, but may be laden with as much geopolitical ambition as profit aspiration. The underbelly of disaster capitalism may, in fact, be an unwitting outcome of international NGO management, as the conclusion in Chapter 6 illustrates with a focus on Aceh.

If catastrophe breeds opportunities for social transformations and economic exploitation, it also generates new social and political openings and space for change. Just eight months after the 2004 tsunami struck Aceh, Indonesia, a peace agreement was finalized between government and rebel forces after more than three decades of deadly conflict. The tsunami did not *cause* the peace agreement, but it certainly created conditions that accelerated its signing.

Dual Disasters

The title of this book, *Dual Disasters,* refers to the devastation of the 2004 Indian Ocean Basin tsunami and the landscapes of deadly conflict that preceded the tsunami. The intersection of humanitarian disasters—one in Sri Lanka and the other in Aceh, Indonesia—with existing conflict in each location constitutes an important conceptual, political, and practical focus for those involved in humanitarianism and post-conflict reconciliation. Aid workers, government policymakers, and international donors have been increasingly aware of the ways in which aid must be conflict sensitive, so that humanitarian interventions avoid fueling war or violence (Culbert 2005). A great deal of work has also focused on the relationship of aid to conflict reduction, yet little is known about what happens when an environmental disaster and a human-made humanitarian crisis overlap spatially and temporally.

This book does not, however, identify a definitive set of links that apply to all dual disasters. Nor does it create a checklist of procedures to approach contexts of multiple disasters, at least not prescriptively so. Rather, the book describes how environmental and economic dimensions of the 2004 tsunami are overlaid with historicized political dimensions of the conflicts that characterized both Sri Lanka and Aceh for decades before the tsunami hit.

In a world increasingly characterized by global warming and environmental degradation, conflict, resource wars, human rights atrocities, and subsequent human displacement are part of humanitarian crises that complicate and exacerbate such processes. Dual disasters, or even multiple disasters, create the most complex of emergencies.

Research for this book began as a study of the patterns of development aid to countries affected by conflict. How do governments of countries at war and donors to them do international aid? Sri Lanka was one of several South Asian focal points for that project when the December 26, 2004, tsunami hit. I suspended my research for a year after the tsunami, as the terrible losses and destruction hit particularly hard in the conflict-affected areas of eastern Sri Lanka. More urgent tasks prevailed, and I along with many others assessed needs and collaborated with relevant agencies to address these issues.

My work with UNICEF in early 2005 involved an assessment of communities affected by both the tsunami and the war in Sri Lanka's North and East. From Jaffna to Akkaraipattu, my colleague and research partner, Dr. Mala de Alwis, and I witnessed firsthand not only the destruction and devastation of the tsunami and the resilience of those who had survived it, but also the neglect of those displaced by the war, but not affected by the tsunami.

My study of aid delivery in conflict zones resumed in 2006, tracing the changes in aid transfers conditioned by the tsunami and its aftermath. I also launched a larger study of the tsunami and its impact at that time on the conflicts in Sri Lanka and Aceh.[4] This book, then, represents the culmination of research over many years. Aided by many collaborators and informants along the way, the findings that follow probe the interaction and impact of dual disasters at multiple scales. As a geographer I have often been asked at what level or scale I conduct my research. Scholars of international relations tend to focus on the scale of the state; quantitative researchers may defer to the scale at which their data have been collected (national, provincial, county), and more qualitative researchers often work at the finer scales of the household or individual subject, conducting livelihood surveys or collecting narratives of displacement from those affected by conflict or other disasters. Yet, "To speak of local, regional, national or even global processes is meaningless— social relations are in fact played out across scales rather than confined within them. Consequently, it makes little sense to privilege any scale as a primary referent for analyzing particular social processes" (Kelly 1999, 381). The approaches chronicled here aim to illustrate that disasters permeate the most intimate and global scales of social and political space:

from the human body and household to the international community and global environment (Mountz and Hyndman 2006).

Geography matters. Those countries that hosted conflict and humanitarian crisis before the tsunami faced a distinct matrix of issues after the tsunami hit. The tsunami was but one more layer of politicized devastation experienced by regions already affected by war. The dynamics of displacement and aid spawned by the tsunami cannot be neatly separated from the relations of dispossession and humanitarian assistance that preceded the tsunami. Understanding the ways in which extant humanitarian crises interact with environmental disasters, such as the tsunami, is critical to planning for such contexts in the future.

While this book draws specifically on post-tsunami fieldwork from Aceh and Sri Lanka, work on other humanitarian crises has influenced my analysis. As a field officer for the UNHCR in Somalia and as a relief worker for CARE in Kenya in the early 1990s, I learned something of what it means to make decisions and deliver assistance during a disaster. My research in Kenyan refugee camps in the mid-1990s, and my work with NGOs in the refugee-serving sector in Canada since that time, have cultivated a deep curiosity about the potential links between conflict zones and their broader environments in general.

Imperial Humanitarianism?

When asked why the 2004 tsunami in the Indian Ocean Basin attracted so much more attention than the devastating Pakistan earthquake that occurred eight months afterward in 2005, one international aid agency official in Colombo remarked that the magnitude of the tsunami was unprecedented (Grundy-Warr and Sidaway 2006). "This disaster was also very much a media opportunity where visuals of women caught up on trees, the plight of children [and such] were shown so freely. As one informant interviewed said, it was almost as if destruction came to the sitting room" (Sri Lanka interview #103, 2007).

Indeed, as anthropologist Pradeep Jeganathan (2005) notes,

At first, it seems silly to ask why so much philanthropy followed the *tsunami*. With so much death, destruction and dislocation there was great need and, obviously, generosity follows need, one might say. . . . The first reason's a little elusive it seems. . . . Michael Ondaatje puts it this way in *Anil's Ghost:*

> American movies, English books—remember how they all end?' Gemini had asked that night. 'The American or Englishman gets on a plane and leaves. That's it. The camera leaves with him. He looks out of the window at Mombassa or Vietnam or Jakarta, someplace he can look through the clouds. The tired hero. . . . The war, to all purposes, is over. . . ."

Well the second reason is simple, really. Natural disasters generate more generosity than (hu)man made ones. No one is to blame in earthquakes and floods, the victims are innocent. In a *tsunami,* the victims are pure and blameless as babies. Charity pours in, to save the children.

Such a politics of blame may explain why some humanitarian crises, such as HIV/AIDS and war-related famine, are less popular with funders. Apparently random environmental disasters are not linked to individual actions or volition. Blamelessness of victims combined with witnessing the related death, loss, and destruction can create fear among those witnesses who are donors to the tsunami. Disasters can precipitate fear and trauma in the societies in which they occur. Responses to disasters, however genuine, are never immune from politicization.

The stark witnessing of blameless "white death," the acute loss of life among white people from the global North, that occurred on television screens worldwide may also account for the generous gifts of money for those affected by the tsunami (Olds, Sidaway, and Sparke 2005). Media coverage of the victims and survivors of the tsunami, many of them Euro-American tourists, generated a frightening sentiment among audiences in the global North that "it could have been me." Yet less than 1% of tsunami fatalities affected tourists (Cosgrave 2007). These transnational media experiences of fear, empathy, and horror led to the single greatest outpouring of international aid for a single humanitarian crisis. Overall, more than $13 billion was pledged, with more than $5 billion coming from private individuals and companies.

One might speak of *duel* disasters as much as *dual* disasters. Existing conditions of war can exacerbate tensions in the wake of another humanitarian disaster, as in Sri Lanka, or a crisis such as the tsunami can accelerate progress toward peace, as in the case of Aceh, Indonesia. Probing the tensions and agreements that have emerged in these two locations and analyzing them in the context of humanitarian assistance constitute the chapters that follow.

Notes

1. Jeffrey Simpson's (2010) coverage of Haiti suffers from this approach. While Simpson observes that the twenty-nine-year dictatorship of Haiti had a negative effect on its current status, he dwells on its indicators rather than examining the country's struggles and how it arrived at such a low place. He observes that Haiti lost 15% of the value of its economy during the tropical storms and hurricanes of 2008. Per capita income is CAD$660 (Canadian dollars), the lowest in the Western Hemisphere. Before the quake only 11% of Haitians had running water. Life expectancy is sixty-one years. Haiti ranks 149 out of 182 countries on the UN Human Development Index. In short, an account of the present that is not historicized is not helpful. It attributes Haiti's failures to its people, however implicitly.

2. Yet for almost two decades the World Bank and International Monetary Fund have insisted that poverty reduction measures must be decided by borrowers themselves. This has taken the form of Poverty Reduction Strategy Papers (PRSPs) that are ostensibly written by countries desperate to borrow in collaboration with their civil society and staff at these banks.

3. See the petition and a partial translation below at http://www.nytimes.com/interactive/2009/05/06/world/asia/06quake.document.html (accessed January 25, 2010).

4. I also joined a research team that probed tsunami politics and practices in both countries, led by Sri Lankan anthropologist Malathi de Alwis, funded by the International Development Research Centre, a Canadian agency.

2

Siting Conflict and Peace in Post-Tsunami Sri Lanka and Aceh, Indonesia

What effect did the 2004 tsunami in the Indian Ocean Basin have on the existing contexts of conflict and peace in Aceh and Sri Lanka? This chapter aims to analyze prevailing humanitarian narratives as well as certain policies that were politicized in the context of conflict, human displacement, and post-tsunami response in both places. First, government imposition of buffer zones as post-tsunami safety measures in both Sri Lanka and Aceh incited tensions, although they were negotiated in very different ways. Second, the development of policy and the implementation of bodies for aid distribution proved highly contentious, but uniquely so in each location. Disparities in treatment between tsunami-affected and conflict-affected persons in both places are also analyzed, a theme I return to in more detail in Chapter 6.

The specific geographical and historical context in which disaster strikes is critical to the meanings it creates. For example, Michael Renner (2006b) notes that in Aceh the *ulamas* (Islamic theologians) blamed women for the tsunami, calling them "female sinners" whose dress and lack of modesty were not morally appropriate prior to the disaster. In 2010 a senior Iranian cleric blamed women's immodest dress for earthquakes, among them the disaster in Bam, Iran, in 2003 (Associated Press 2010). In Aceh, sharia law predated the tsunami, but the sharia police to enforce that law did not emerge in Aceh until afterward. A specifically gendered cultural politics underpins understandings of the tsunami. In May 2010 the regional government in Aceh implemented an ordinance that bans tight-fitting clothing on women. A woman who violates the code would be required to wear one of twenty thousand government-issue skirts. After three offenses, her apparel would be confiscated (*Jakarta Post* 2010). A careful anthropological analysis of these highly gendered narratives of propriety and responsibility remains to be done, but it is clear that the ways in which blame was assigned were very quickly politicized.

Likewise, stories circulated that Javanese government soldiers were smoking and drinking at an important religious site at the shoreline in Banda Aceh the night before the waves hit. Their morally inferior behavior was thought by some to incur the wrath of God in the form of the tsunami. In contrast, at Lok Nga, a village hard-hit by the tsunami just west of Banda Aceh, a mosque survived where no other structure did. Many saw this as another divine sign, and the mosque has been restored to its former glory (see Figure 2.1).

This chapter juxtaposes conditions of conflict, devastation, and response in Sri Lanka and Aceh, Indonesia, the two most acutely affected regions in the wake of the 2004 tsunami. The existing research on the intersection of "man-made" versus "natural" disasters is considerable (Kelman and Gaillard 2007; Wisner et al. 2004). A number of geographers

Figure 2.1 Restored Mosque, West of Banda Aceh

(Lawson 2005; Marston 2005; Olds, Sidaway, and Sparke 2005; Stokke 2005; Korf 2005; Le Billon and Waizenegger 2007; Kleinfeld 2007; Gaillard et al. 2008) and other social scientists (Jeganathan 2005; Kennedy et al. 2008; among others) have also taken up different elements of the humanitarian question since the tsunami hit.

Perhaps the most important caveat framing this chapter is that geographically diverse processes and politics produce the particular patterns and examples provided below. As geographer Matthew Sparke (2005, xiv) remarks, "Any assumption about geography either as a result of or as a basis or container of spatial relations for other social relations always risks fetishizing a particular spatial arrangement and ignoring ongoing processes of spatial production, negotiation, and contestation." Put another way, to overstate any geographical similarities between two tsunami-affected sites risks ignoring the multiscalar processes and human relationships that have generated distinctive histories of struggle and sovereignty, and also distinctive disaster-response policies. Contextualizing these spaces of disaster is an important departure point.

Each conflict has historically and geopolitically distinct antecedents, resulting in different post-disaster policy contexts and unique challenges on the ground. Whereas the tsunami in Sri Lanka was followed by renewed fighting, the end of a ceasefire agreement, and a brutal finale to military conflict in May 2009, people in the province of Aceh, Indonesia, have enjoyed the fruits of a 2005 peace agreement that has created greater autonomy from the central government in Jakarta than ever before.

The people of Aceh have long fought for autonomy from colonial rulers as well as from the centralized government of Indonesia. In Sri Lanka the political project of a separate breakaway Tamil state by the LTTE has waned since the government of Sri Lanka (GoSL) defeated Tiger rebels in a deadly standoff in April and May 2009. Yet this post-independence war, stemming from the anti-Tamil pogroms of 1983 in Colombo, stretched over a period of more than twenty-five years. Calls for a separate state in Sri Lanka can be traced to the early 1970s when constitutional reforms alienated Tamils in what was formerly Ceylon. Both conflicts were in their third consecutive decade when the tsunami hit.

Today, political and economic conditions in these two affected areas are dramatically different from one another and starkly similar. In Aceh the Indonesian government signed a peace agreement with the Free Aceh

Movement (Gerakan Aceh Merdeka, GAM) in August 2005, just eight
months after the tsunami. It still holds in 2010. In Sri Lanka political developments since the tsunami intensified the country's prolonged political crisis (Uyangoda 2005), leading to the abrogation of a 2002 ceasefire
agreement in 2008 by the Sri Lankan government in the wake of rebel
attacks. The deadly battle between government troops and rebel Tamil
Tigers led to the government declaring military victory in May 2009.
Tamil civilians were literally caught in the middle of this fighting, with
tens of thousands of civilians killed in the first five months of that year
(International Crisis Group [ICG] 2010). While civilian deaths rose precipitously after the tsunami in Sri Lanka, Aceh witnessed a somewhat
precarious but continuous period of peace.

Despite this crude political contrast of war and peace after the
tsunami, both places exhibited political tensions and resentment in the
wake of reconstruction. The landscapes of conflict and displacement that
preceded the tsunami cannot simply be erased. Rather, a variegated,
politicized layer of disaster and aid overlays these earlier disparities, histories, and geographies of displacement. Distinct societal cleavages, political tensions, and economic disparities between Aceh and Sri Lanka
predate the tsunami, so any juxtaposition must avoid direct comparison
that might eclipse the nuanced differences and dynamics that historically and geographically constitute each place.

The Politics of Displacement: Pre-Tsunami

The devastation of the tsunami overlays longstanding geopolitical tensions, struggles for resources, and politics of displacement (Nah and Bunnell 2005; Hyndman and de Alwis 2004). In what follows I briefly
sketch the political backdrop to conflict in both Aceh and Sri Lanka,
setting the stage for the tsunami politics that ensued after the fateful
waves of December 26, 2004, hit Aceh and Sri Lanka.

Indonesia

Sentiments around sovereignty and Islam as a national project in Aceh
are more pronounced than in most other parts of Indonesia. When
Dutch forces recaptured Indonesia in 1946 after Japan's defeat in the

Second World War, Aceh remained the only free region of the archipelago (Waizenegger 2007). The Acehnese people and politicians both broadly supported the creation of the Indonesian Republic in principle, in large part because they believed it would be an Islamic state and Aceh would be granted special provincial status (Aspinall 2007). The creation of a secular and centralized Federal Republic of Indonesia in 1949 was seen as a betrayal of Aceh's loyalty and support, sowing seeds of rebellion.

In response to this dissidence, the first president of Indonesia, Sukarno, granted Aceh separate provincial status in 1959, and gave it the status of a "special region" (*Daerah Istimewa*) in 1961 to pacify the Acehnese. But Sukarno's political nemesis and a general in his military, Suharto, stoked discontent during his rule, beginning in the mid-1960s. Suharto succeeded in forcing Sukarno from office in 1967, and took over the presidency. Feelings of exploitation soared among the Acehnese in 1971 when huge oil and natural gas deposits were discovered near Lhokseumawe and Lhoksukon in North Aceh. Exploration was followed by the construction of a major refinery, financed as a joint venture between the Indonesian state-owned Pertamina and ExxonMobil (Renner 2006a).

Among the companies that had sought to run the refinery was Doral International, a conglomerate owned by the Acehnese businessman Teungku Hasan di Tiro (Waizenegger and Hyndman 2010). Di Tiro is a descendant of the last sultan of Aceh and a direct descendant of Teuku Cik di Tiro, a famous Acehnese national hero during the Aceh War of 1873–1903, so his defeat in the oil deal was interpreted as a renewed expression of the unjust Javanese economic exploitation and domination of the province. The confiscation of villagers' land without compensation by the government of Indonesia and the deployment of as many as 5,000 troops to protect ExxonMobil from the emerging rebel force also fueled Acehnese nationalism (Renner 2006a).

Jim Glassman (2005) argues that the Indonesian state was partially to blame for the Aceh region's susceptibility to death and destruction during the tsunami. Despite Aceh's natural-resource wealth, Javanese sub-imperialism and the US-backed rule of President Suharto had led to the Acehnese "people leading marginal lives and surviving on marginal resources" (166). This confluence of Cold War geopolitics, in which the West provided considerable backing for the Indonesian military and Java-centric governance to ensure the flow of energy revenues from Aceh to Jakarta, generated a skewed political economy in the region well into the post–Cold War period. Such political currents continued even in the wake of the tsunami when, as Glassman reports, GAM honored the cease-fire while the Indonesian military continued to attack GAM strongholds.

GAM has been fighting for Aceh's independence from Indonesia since 1976. After a number of attacks by GAM in 1989–1990—a period of massive human rights violations on both sides—the Indonesian military launched a massive counterinsurgency operation in Aceh Province that continued on and off into 2005 (Nah and Bunnell 2005). In December 2002 a cessation of hostilities agreement was signed, drastically reducing the number of killings (Renner 2006b). Yet by May 2003, in response to renewed Acehnese calls for a share of resource revenues, the government of Indonesia declared a state of emergency in Aceh (Hedman 2005), and the region was highly militarized by the Indonesian government, which installed more than 40,000 additional troops to forcibly relocate insurgents. Well before the tsunami, more than 300,000 people had already been displaced by conflict, violence, and counterinsurgency.

In October 2004 Susilo Bambang Yudhoyono became president of Indonesia (he was reelected in 2009), with a pledge to seek peace in Aceh. In December 2004 the tsunami hit Aceh. Just eight months later, after five rounds of talks, a peace agreement known as the memorandum of understanding (MoU) was signed in August 2005. It secured troop withdrawal, disarmament of rebels, more energy revenues for the Aceh region, and greater autonomy for local government in Aceh. As the wording of the peace agreement specifically states, "The parties are deeply convinced that only the peaceful settlement of the conflict will enable the rebuilding of Aceh after the tsunami disaster on 26 December 2004 to progress and succeed." The newly elected president put it this way:

> The tsunami produced an overwhelming moral, political, economic, social imperative to end the conflict. . . . I was criticized by those who did not see any benefit from renewed talks with GAM. But I was more concerned about the judgment of history for missing this rare window of opportunity to resolve the conflict. (Yudhoyono 2006)

The principles of peace outlined in 2005, although somewhat diluted due to resistance by hardliners, were passed into law governing Aceh in July 2006 (Renner 2006a).

Sri Lanka

In Sri Lanka, a war characterized as one of violent competing nationalisms between the secessionist LTTE and the government of Sri Lanka's armed forces has been waged for more than twenty-five years (Jayawardena and de Alwis 1996). Contemporary Sri Lanka is an expression of a long history and geography of struggle well-documented by Sri Lankan and Sri Lankanist scholars (Abeysekera and Gunasinghe 1987; Jeganathan and Ismail 1995; Thiruchelvam 1996). At the time of writing, the death toll from the conflict approximates 100,000 in a country of 20 million people. During the ceasefire agreement between the government and the LTTE, signed in February 2002, deaths fell noticeably until 2006, when hostilities resumed despite the agreement. In a moment of hope in 2003 a donor conference to finance the reconstruction of war-torn Sri Lanka met in Tokyo; US$4.5 billion was pledged for the Regaining Sri Lanka strategy, one referred to as a "cash for peace approach" (Jeyeraj 2005; Bastian 2007a).

After the 2004 tsunami in Sri Lanka, and quite separate from the US$4.5 billion pledged the year before, the World Bank assessed the cost of reconstruction and recovery at approximately US$1.5 billion. How to allocate these funds emerged as one of the biggest hurdles faced by the government and the LTTE. A joint mechanism to distribute international aid to tsunami-affected areas was proposed at an international donor forum in May 2005 (Kleinfeld 2007). Called the Post-Tsunami Operational Management Structure, or P-TOMS, the joint mechanism was a memorandum of understanding that set out terms for a working relationship between the government of Sri Lanka and the LTTE. P-TOMS included representation from not only the Sri Lankan government and the LTTE but also from Muslim political parties. Muslim communities living along the devastated east coast were disproportionately hit by the tsunami, given their concentration in that region.[1]

Signed in June 2005 the P-TOMS memorandum became a firebrand for political acrimony, galvanizing Sinhalese nationalist sentiment in opposition to it because of the legitimacy it potentially conferred on the militant Tamil nationalists, the LTTE. The Sinhala nationalist *Janatha Vimukthi Peramuna* (JVP) party, in a coalition with the sitting government, petitioned the Supreme Court in July 2005 on the grounds that P-TOMS violated the rights of Sri Lankan citizens and the territorial integrity of the state for the following reasons (Kleinfeld 2007, 179):

- The LTTE was a terrorist organization, not a governmental entity that could legitimately participate in such an agreement.
- The committees described in P-TOMS were governmental in nature and could not legally do the work they were charged to do without constitutional changes.
- Donor funds were funds of the Republic and could not be controlled by an outside agency like the World Bank (as was outlined in the MoU).
- Treatment of persons within the tsunami disaster zone (TDZ) discriminated against tsunami-affected persons outside the TDZ.

Humanitarian aid continued to flow regardless of the fate of P-TOMS, but disbursement of the big pots of money for reconstruction went to the government. If P-TOMS had succeeded, it might have served as a blueprint for the constitutional change required for lasting peace in Sri Lanka. However, it did not. The Supreme Court largely agreed with the plaintiff, and the MoU was never adopted. Prime Minister Mahinda Rajapakse ran for president later that year on n anti–P-TOMS platform and won by a slim margin (Bastian 2007b). With his presidency and its consolidated alliance with Sinhalese hardliners, such as the JVP, violence increased notably in Sri Lanka.

By early 2008 the government of Sri Lanka ended the ceasefire agreement, and the Nordic monitors of the Sri Lanka Monitoring Mission (SLMM) left the country. Bus bombs and suicide attacks in public areas, like those witnessed throughout the 1990s, resumed. Between December 2004 and June 2007 more than 6,000 people were killed (Kleinfeld 2007). As noted above, the ICG (2010) released a report in May 2010 stating that 30,000 or more civilians died in the fighting during the last few weeks of the conflict, and that most were killed by government fire. The agency found war crimes committed by both parties, and credible evidence that government security forces intentionally shelled civilians, hospitals, and humanitarian operations, while the LTTE refused to allow civilians to leave the conflict zone and shot those who tried. In May the war was over. The number of people who died in the tsunami was lower than the number killed in the fighting during the first five months of 2009.

Political Geographies of Displacement:
Post-Tsunami Buffer Zone Policies

The tsunami generally worsened the humanitarian, social, and economic situation of people living in both the province of Aceh and in Sri Lanka. The regions most affected—Western Aceh on the northern part of Sumatra Island and the eastern coast of Sri Lanka[2]—both have long histories of exclusion, poverty, and conflict, yet the infusion of aid and the patterns it took created very different dynamics in each location. In both Sri Lanka and Aceh, money to rebuild houses was plentiful, but coordinating housing reconstruction and securing the land on which to build new homes was more elusive (Centre for Policy Alternatives 2005; Renner 2006b). In both countries, buffer zone policies that initially prohibited rebuilding homes near the sea generated another wave of displacement, politicizing humanitarian aid.

The buffer zone policy displaced yet again those who had already lost their homes through the dislocation of conflict and then the tsunami. This fueled resentment among minority ethnic groups, namely Muslims and Tamils, a theme I return to in the next chapter. Some Sri Lankan commentators have argued that the policy was a politicized land-grab on the part of the government in one of the most densely populated countries in the world.[3]

Aceh, in contrast, experienced a different kind of politicization in relation to the buffer zones. There, resentment based on unequal treatment of tsunami-affected and war-affected people emerged early on as a more important issue than buffer zones, a finding explored in detail in Chapter 6. I sketch each of these contexts in turn.

Fostering Conflict, Buffering Blame in Sri Lanka

The setback or buffer zones declared by the government of Sri Lanka represented a state-sponsored dislocation for many people along the east coast who had already been affected by the dual disasters of war and the huge waves. Before the tsunami, during periods of intense conflict, many Muslim and Tamil communities found sanctuary on these unoccupied shores—narrow strips of land between the sea and the more inland lagoons, called littoral, or *eluvankaral,* in Tamil (see Figure 2.2). The hinterland, or *paduvaankaral,* farther inland from the lagoons is occupied

Figure 2.2 Map of Sri Lanka, East Coast

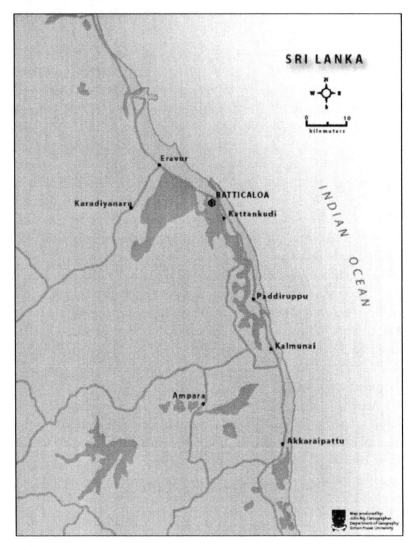

largely by Sinhalese, the majority ethnic group, who were resettled from other parts of the country through government colonization schemes during the nationalist periods of the 1950s and 1970s (Jeyeraj 2005).

From the moment the Sri Lankan government announced the buffer zones, cries of ethnic discrimination could be heard. Muslim communities were over-represented as a proportion of the general population in the hardest-hit parts of the eastern Ampara district and therefore over-represented in terms of the death and destruction wreaked in that area. So when the government announced a two-hundred-meter no-build zone along the east coast in contrast to a narrower one-hundred-meter buffer zone along the south coast where homes of the Sinhala majority are most numerous, Tamil and Muslim groups called the buffer zones unfair and a sign of ethnic prejudice (K. de Alwis 2005).

> When the buffer zone made its entrance after the waves had left behind the destruction [in January 2005], it was known by another name, less popular—set back zone. It most certainly has lived up to that title. (A. Perera 2005)

The no-build areas served to reproduce extant patterns of discrimination against minority Tamils and Muslims in the wake of the tsunami and to fuel mistrust.

The high population density and scarcity of land also made the setbacks in the East and South highly contentious. The president's office announced that the government would identify lands closest to the affected villages and would build a house for "every affected house owner who lived within the said 100 meters" (Sambandan 2005). Owners of homes that were inside the buffer zone "will retain the ownership of his original land" and the government "will not in any way claim ownership to such property." Moreover, the owner would be "entitled to appropriate the land (within the 100-metre-zone) as he wishes, except building on it." The government would "extend patronage to planting coconut or any other suitable crop in those lands" (Sambandan 2005). This was easier said than done, given the relatively high density of Sri Lanka. Land reforms during the 1970s did allow the government to acquire 400,000 hectares of land. Nonetheless, this posed an obstacle to reconstruction and delayed home-building for those with property inside the buffer zones.

Land within the buffer zone could still be used for business purposes, including hotels, a particularly important resource for tourism operators in Sinhala-dominated beach areas of southern Sri Lanka (MONLAR and ANRHR [Movement for National Land and Agricultural Reform and Alliance for Protection of National Resources and

Human Rights] 2005). In the end, hotels were rebuilt not even ten meters from the high-tide watermark (Figure 2.3). So, while Sri Lankan citizens could no longer reside along the south coast, tourists could. The terms of rebuilding and compensation were also controversial. Owners of homes and squatters alike could have houses rebuilt with aid either from the government or from an approved NGO, but tenants renting from owners got nothing except the right to rent again if and when owners rebuilt (Centre for Policy Alternatives 2005).

The logic, or lack thereof, behind the decision making showed early signs of strain. If public safety were the primary aim, the buffer zones should have been equivalent for all areas (Institute for Policy Studies 2005). Hotels and other tourism ventures should not have been permitted in the danger zone. If humanitarian principles were paramount, tenants as well as owners would have been compensated. The effectiveness of buffer zones is debatable. The lack of evidence to rationalize the buffer zones is striking. For example, on March 28, 2005, an earthquake that registered 8.7 in force rocked southern Sri Lanka. Then president Chandrika Kumaratunga stated that the mere occurrence of the earthquake, which did

Figure 2.3 Hotel Rebuilt on Unawatuna Beach, South Coast, Sri Lanka

not create a tsunami, was a logical rationale for the buffer zone: "The people now should realize that the government, bearing in mind all allegation leveled against it, has acted prudently with a vision and in a responsible manner" (Associated Press 2005). Meanwhile, an opposition Member of Parliament (MP) and former minister, Ravi Karunanayake, retorted that in his riding of Crows Island, fifteen hundred National Housing Development Authority houses went underwater in the tsunami, despite the fact that they were built more than one hundred meters from the shoreline—proof, he said, that the buffer zone would be ineffectual. By denying access to previously occupied territories and by doing so in an inconsistent and biased fashion, the buffer zone policy further victimized tsunami survivors and fueled political interpretations that intensified ethno-national tensions. Instead of helping with renewal, buffer zones have been, as Sri Lanka's World Bank representative Peter Harrold notes, the single greatest barrier to progress in housing reconstruction (cited in Dias 2006).

The buffer zones proved to be a political hot potato for President Chandrika Kumaratunga, whose term ended in November 2005. At that time, then prime minister Mahinda Rajapakse was elected president of Sri Lanka. Rajapakse quickly distanced himself from the Kumaratunga presidency, first by changing his predecessor's government tsunami response body from the Task Force to Rebuild the Nation (TAFREN) to the Reconstruction and Development Agency (RADA). Then, through RADA, he announced in February 2006 that the buffer zone setback standards would be relaxed and that the setback standards of the Coastal Zone Management Plan of 1997 would be revived (*Sunday Times* 2006). The Advisory Council of the Coast Conservation Department had approved some exemptions from the buffer zone policy even before Kumaratunga left office (Cassim 2005), but by invoking the Coastal Zone Management Plan, President Rajapakse appeared to have scientific reason on his side. The plan had been adopted but not enforced by various Sri Lankan governments since the 1980s and was based on protecting the coast and its inhabitants through appropriate vegetation. The 1997 version allows for setbacks between 35 meters and 125 meters from the permanent vegetation boundary, depending on coastal conditions. That the plan predated the tsunami and appeared to the public to be based on environmental science depoliticized the buffer zone controversy, an issue I revisit in the next chapter.

Aceh's Blueprint and Buffers

In Aceh the size of buffer zones announced by the government was sub-stantially greater at the outset: "Within a two-kilometer area from the shore, we will avoid building houses, offices, markets and shopping cen-ters," declared Mawardi Nurdea, head of Aceh's urban planning and housing authority in February 2005 (Sukarsono 2005). Fishers were ex-empt from this policy, and could live four hundred meters back from the sea. Protests soon developed owing to the top-down policy and lack of consultation with those displaced by the tsunami (Leckie 2005). Donors and beneficiaries alike demanded community-based consultations. The blanket policy of buffer zones was rolled back, as was evident during a field visit I made in June 2007 to Lok Nga, about ten kilometers from Banda Aceh on the hardest-hit west coast. There, an entire village has been rebuilt not more than four hundred meters back from the sea around the large mosque shown earlier that largely survived the tsunami.

In both Aceh and Sri Lanka, the buffer zone proclamations initially represented the position of central governments that then evolved and became more geographically tailored and politically sensitive. However, in Aceh the central government retained a stronger role in the delivery of post-tsunami aid through its master plan or blueprint for reconstruc-tion. This stands in contrast to the more decentralized and arguably politicized planning that eventually took place at the provincial and dis-trict levels in Sri Lanka.

In both Sri Lanka and Aceh, international NGOs took on a major role in disaster relief and began staking claims to particular projects and places. While efforts to help were well-intentioned, the result was a confusing com-petition among NGOs that had their own organizational agendas. Coor-dination efforts began in the president's office, but it soon became clear that such centralization of control was not politically popular; provincial and local levels would have to become involved. In Sri Lanka, provincial civil servants met with INGO staff late into the night most evenings early in 2005, trying to allocate projects in affected areas to different organi-zations, to make peace with warring NGOs that claimed similar areas to rebuild, and to avoid duplicating services.

In Aceh, too, INGOs competed with one another for space to conduct their humanitarian projects (Renner 2006b). INGOs provided essential resources and were successful in some of the reconstruction projects they undertook, yet their capacity to spend all the funds that they had and directly oversee the work that needed to be done was, at times, in question. For example, the new houses provided by the Turkish Red Crescent Society near Banda Aceh are considered among the best built of the reconstruction effort. However, many are vacant due to poor water supply, a problem in location that might have been avoided with more local consultation. Much criticism of the INGO community ensued for its initial failure to consult with national and local counterparts (Couldrey and Morris 2005).

The ownership of these private, if nonprofit, international organizations in relation to the elected Sri Lankan governing authorities remains an important issue identified by John Cosgrave's (2007) report for the Tsunami Evaluation Coalition (TEC).[4]

> Those who own a process control it; they decide which priorities and policies apply. Ownership can be vested in all levels of society, from the central government to the village committee. . . . Ownership has come to the fore in development literature in the last two decades, but has received little attention in relief. (17)

Accountability is another issue. It refers in this context to organizations held responsible for their actions to a particular group, such as the affected population, the affected government, donors, taxpayers, or other humanitarian agencies. Transparency and feedback mechanisms on actions taken are two key elements of accountability (ibid.). Most important, the first recommendation of the TEC relates to both:

> The international humanitarian community needs a fundamental reorientation from supplying aid to supporting and facilitating communities' own relief and recovery priorities. (Cosgrave 2007, 22)

The first responders to the tsunami were members of the public who lived nearby. In Aceh, Red Cross volunteers were also on the scene, but the response during the first two days of assistance was largely community-based. Maintaining that relationship of ownership and accountability by communities to their members is one that should have remained intact, but did not once international humanitarian organizations arrived.

The actions of well-intentioned INGOs, with headquarters in Europe, Australia, Japan, and North America, may have been accepted by the tsunami-affected countries as the price to be paid for humanitarian assistance, but the issues of ownership and accountability remain open. Aid is never as impartial as it claims to be.

The pursuit of private for-profit interests in humanitarian reconstruction is also a concern. In both Sri Lanka and Aceh the rationale for the buffer zones was public safety, but as soon as the policy was announced in Aceh, private-sector developers and other political insiders began jockeying for a piece of the post-tsunami reconstruction pie outlined in the blueprint (Renner 2006b), attempting to profit from what Naomi Klein (2007) has called "disaster capitalism." In Aceh critics have raised concerns and expressed suspicion about a new superhighway built (not rebuilt) along Aceh's sparsely populated west coast after the tsunami. In February 2008, news articles revealed that an Indonesian state agency said it had discovered potentially massive hydrocarbon reserves off Aceh's west coast (Dow Jones Newswires 2008). Further evidence of extraction potential is being sought, but "the reserve might reach a minimum of 107 billion barrels and a maximum of 320 billion barrels of oil or gas. By comparison, the proven reserve of Saudi Arabia is around 264 billion barrels, the largest in the world, while the Banyu Urip block in Cepu, Central Java, contains around 450 million barrels" (*Jakarta Post* 2008). Speculation that the discovery of reserves off Aceh's west coast requires such highway infrastructure and that international donors may have known about the reserves even before the tsunami occurred is circulating. Again, further investigation and material evidence is needed to prove the disaster capitalism thesis in this context.

Rich Cousin, Poor Cousin: Tsunami Aid Politics and Post-Conflict Integration

Just as disaster is never simply "natural" (N. Smith 2006), "reconstruction is never just a physical task" (Renner 2006b, 13). In Sri Lanka along the eastern coast, tsunami-affected people were also intensely conflict-affected, especially in terms of geographical displacement. However, in Aceh, those intensely affected by conflict largely did not overlap with those devastated by the tsunami, an issue discussed in more detail in Chapter 6. In Sri Lanka, communities displaced by conflict that were not affected by the tsunami have been largely ignored, at least in terms of tsunami aid. One distinction between conflict-affected people in Sri Lanka and in Aceh is that the latter group experienced a dramatic loss of livelihood after the 2005 peace agreement between the government of Indonesia and GAM (MoU 2005) that required rebel fighters to give up their weapons and demobilize. Very few funds for their reintegration have been forthcoming, yet the MoU (2005) does make a provision for reintegration in section 3.2.3:

> GoI and the authorities of Aceh will take measures to assist persons who have participated in GAM activities to facilitate their reintegration into the civil society. These measures include economic facilitation to former combatants, pardoned political prisoners and affected civilians. A Reintegration Fund under the administration of the authorities of Aceh will be established.

The MoU goes on to say that all former combatants will receive an allocation of farmland, employment, or adequate social security. However, the number of combatants listed in the MoU (3,000 military troops) is widely considered to be an undercount (Renner 2006a). Hence, the funds for reintegration are paltry. While some senior GAM leaders did receive a peace dividend from the 2005 agreement in the form of jobs with the government agency for reconstruction (Rehabilitation and Reconstruction Agency for Aceh and Nias [*Badan Rehabilitasi dan Rekonstruksi*, BRR]), the benefits were bestowed among a small, elite minority.

In Aceh, deep-seated resentment has emerged based on the uneven distribution of funds between GAM commanders and foot soldiers. Dramatically different levels of aid were available to tsunami survivors as compared to demobilized soldiers. As Ida Wati, former GAM rebel, stated, "The tsunami victims were the lucky ones. . . . At least they got help" (cited in Honorine 2007). A great number of GAM—including combatants, noncombatants, and prisoners given amnesty—are frustrated:

> We also find a lot of dissatisfaction among GAM themselves. Their job is to fight, so now they are unemployed. They face problems feeding their families. There is a reaction to the fancy cars and "Indonesian"

behavior high-ranking GAM have shown. GAM commanders got
reintegration funds, but foot soldiers got nothing. There is a lot of
resentment. (Aceh interview #202, June 2007)

Reintegration of former combatants into civil society is a highly political matter, with the potential for strong politicization. The inadequacies
of reintegration and resources to accomplish it are explored in more
depth in Chapter 6, but it is a problem in Aceh that distinguishes it from
Sri Lanka, where military conflict has ended but the cessation of hostilities remains incomplete in many parts of the country. In Sri Lanka, Tamil
Tigers were killed or they were captured and encamped by government
troops as part of a large civilian population; some hid as civilians or fled
abroad. There was no formal peace process that created pathways for
them to return to Sri Lankan society. I return in chapter 6 to Aceh and
the dramatically disparate geographies of aid to those affected by the
tsunami and those affected by the conflict.

The 2004 Tsunami: Impetus to Peace or War?

This chapter has provided an overview and analyzed the broad contours
of post-tsunami political landscapes. In Aceh evidence that the tsunami
accelerated and facilitated peace has been documented. In Sri Lanka the
history and dynamics of conflict since the 2004 disaster are very different, but they intensified the country's prolonged political crisis, rather
than alleviating it as in Aceh. Policies ostensibly aimed at improving public safety in the event of another tsunami instead created antagonism.
Government buffer zone policies to restrict rebuilding in designated setback areas along the coast proved highly contentious in both environments, but their outcomes were very different. In Sri Lanka the buffer
zones arguably fueled ethno-national tensions, if not outright conflict.
Protests of this top-down policy imposed by government were met with
a new, more consultative approach to post-tsunami reconstruction.

Likewise, various policy mechanisms, or blueprints, for *distributing*
post-tsunami aid also proved to have significance beyond the mere logistics of reconstruction. In Aceh the peace agreement specified that
some government jobs at the reconstruction agency (BRR) would be

made available to ex-GAM members as part of a peace dividend. The blueprint created both the BRR agency for reconstruction and the Aceh Peace-Reintegration Agency (*Badan Reintegrasi Damai Aceh,* BRA) for reintegration, with formal (if contested) mandates and timelines for operation. In Sri Lanka no joint mechanism was ever agreed upon. The P-TOMS MoU was a promising compromise while it lasted. Representation by Muslims, the LTTE rebels, and the Sri Lankan government made it an explosive but potentially radical intervention to enable humanitarian aid to be delivered. The political geographies of post-tsunami Aceh and Sri Lanka are thus, in one sense, a study in contrasts.

In December 2006 Irwandi Yusuf, a former rebel leader with GAM, won the election for governor of Aceh Province—an election won as a concession to GAM in the peace agreement. Irwandi, who surprised most observers by being elected at all (he won 38% of the vote), was in jail for treason when the Indian Ocean tsunami crashed into Aceh in 2004. Unlike most of his prison mates, he was able to swim to safety, escaping his cell only after the waves hit (Mydans 2007). New provincial elections in 2009 also balloted in favor of former GAM rebels and their allies, yet resentment still brews among ex-GAM rank-and-file members who lost livelihoods with the cessation of hostilities. Economic disparities between the conflict-affected and the tsunami-affected also fuel the tension.

All of this devolution of power to the province of Aceh is a far cry from Sri Lanka, where talk of a more federal, devolved state has gone nowhere over the past two decades. The LTTE did stop reiterating its wishes for a separate state after the ceasefire agreement and P-TOMS brought together all the players required for more sustained talks of peace and constitutional change. But this process did not go any further. While the military conflict may have ended in 2009, reconciliation and peace among the asymmetrical, competing nationalisms in Sri Lanka are conspicuously absent.

The policies employed and political tensions generated by international aid organizations, national governments, and those affected by the dual disasters cannot be forced into a strictly comparative framework. The 2004 tsunami and related disaster aid clearly has had no single effect on existing conflicts and humanitarian crises in Aceh and Sri Lanka. The tsunami may have expanded the political space to negotiate peace and at the same time bred discontent among those required to give up arms, as in the case of Aceh, or it may have catalyzed tensions among ethno-national groups in a war of competing nationalisms, as in Sri Lanka. Tracing these and other stories in more detail is the focus of the chapters that follow.

Notes

1. The density of Sri Lanka is high at 280 persons per square kilometer (725 per square mile), but higher still in the capital city and along the east coast where the tsunami hit. While Muslims make up about 8% of the national population, many are concentrated along this coast; hence they were disproportionately affected.

2. All of the Sri Lankan coastline was affected. The World Bank estimated that 40% of damage was along the east coast, 30% along the southern coast, 20% in the North (another region seriously affected by conflict), and 10% along the west coast.

3. I thank Sunil Bastian for his astute observation on this point.

4. The TEC was established by the Active Learning Network for Accountability and Performance in Humanitarian Action (ALNAP) with three objectives in mind. First, it aimed to improve the quality of humanitarian action and link it to longer-term recovery and development by learning lessons from international responses to the tsunami. Second, it sought to provide accountability to both donor and affected-country populations in relation to the overall response. Third, the Tsunami Evaluation Coalition was tested as an approach and possible model for future collaborative evaluations of humanitarianism (ALNAP 2009).

3

Threats, Fears, and Aid
in Post-Tsunami Sri Lanka

Fear is a visceral response to a perceived threat. It can be a survival mechanism that causes us to retreat from life-threatening situations, or an honest feeling of vulnerability that releases chemicals that put us on alert. Fear can also be exploited or manipulated for political purposes; it is this understanding of fear that I explore in this chapter.

Fear is a potent political resource. It can be used in a variety of ways—to create public consent for tougher security measures, to justify foreign aid in particular locations and not others, to expand border controls, to monitor and punish certain behaviors, to impose health regulations, and so forth. Governments may create and capitalize on fear to expand their control.

In an increasingly globalized world characterized by conflict, human displacement, pandemics, and terrorist attacks, the production and exploitation of fear have far-reaching impacts. Fear can create feelings of nationalism rooted in economic marginalization, loss of territory, and anxieties about invasions of one's home. Some anxieties are, of course, more legitimate than others, as political leaders may create and exploit particular ones for political reasons. Such anxieties give rise to the securitization of fear, whereby feelings of danger are used to underwrite the allocation of resources to fortify borders, manage risk, or take up arms. The securitization of fear and its geopolitical uses and human abuses in the context of disaster, conflict, and human displacement are explored below.

This chapter examines several expressions of fear that have significant implications for broader humanitarian research agendas. First, I explore the ways in which fear is produced for political use in the context of nationalism and in defense of home specifically. Second, I trace how the politics of international aid intersect with fear. Feelings of increased vulnerability at home in donor countries are used to rationalize foreign aid and make it politically relevant. Once a climate of fear has been created, such crises can be offset by aid to locations that represent geopolitical threats. This aid is often compromised in various ways by political agendas and may do as much harm as good. Unraveling the ways in which fear is linked to nationalism in ways that can justify violence, and exclusion is a pressing political and intellectual task.

Finally I probe further the story of the buffer zones and their implementation in post-tsunami Sri Lanka. These setback areas, where home reconstruction was prohibited along the affected coastlines, vividly illustrate how a policy to enhance public safety at a national level stirred, instead, nationalist feelings of discrimination, tension, and fear. Humanitarian remedies that are not consciously conflict-sensitive can unwittingly generate fear and mistrust.

The production of crises—and the fear and xenophobia they instill—remains a pressing concern because it creates legitimate grounds for exceptional interventions (Agamben 1998; Mountz 2004). States often produce or exacerbate crisis and fear to obtain consent for securitization measures. The use of extraordinary measures to secure borders against perceived threats, such as unwanted migrants, is not particularly new. Radhika Mongia (1999) chronicles the ways in which the Canadian government excluded British subjects from India at the turn of the twentieth century through racialized regulations that prevented them from landing, but did not explicitly name race as the rationale. The US Patriot Act, passed after September 11, 2001 (hereafter 9/11), suspended many civil rights in the name of national security. Likewise, the Sri Lankan government maintained a state of emergency even after the war there ended in May 2009 in order to keep Sri Lankan Tamils interned in camps, an act that would have otherwise violated citizenship rights outlined in the Sri Lankan constitution. Fueling fears that there were Tiger rebels among those in the camps, the government was able to create legitimate grounds for this extraordinary measure of containment. Probing the ways in which fear is produced, used, and sometimes reproduced in contexts of disaster and aid is crucial to contesting the harm it can do.

The Production of Fear

> Sleepless in the early hours, you make a nest out of your own fears—
> there must have been survival advantage in dreaming up bad outcomes
> and scheming to avoid them. This trick of dark imagining is one legacy
> of natural selection in a dangerous world. (McEwan 2005, 39)

This passage in McEwan's *Saturday* obliquely illustrates the work
that fear does in a post-9/11 world. His protagonist, a London-based
surgeon who lives within sight of Heathrow Airport, sees a plane on fire.
Immediately he thinks that it must be a terrorist plot, an assumption
embedded in a specific geopolitical imagination.

> The expansion of fear also comes from geopolitical fearmongering and
> intense conflicts from Darfur to Iraq. It comes from our growing ap-
> prehensions about inequality, social injustice and political instability
> across the globe. . . . Fear plays many roles in consolidating the nation
> and in legitimating government actions. (Lawson 2005)

Fear is an emotional reaction to a perceived danger. It emerges from feelings of vulnerability or apprehension. During the war in Sri Lanka, parents in the Eastern Province kept their kids home from school at times for
fear they would be abducted and recruited by the LTTE to fight for the
rebel cause. The tsunami created new fears, and responses to it fed existing anxieties about injustice, marginalization, and preferential treatment.

Making Nationalism

Fear can be both an antecedent to the rise of nationalism and a byprod-
uct of it. With nationalism comes a perception of vulnerability to other
nations. Vulnerability cultivates fear, which is sometimes used for political purposes. Fear has been incited through geostrategic tactics of nationalism that stir feelings of unity but also of common threat and
potential loss of homeland. In his 1989 speeches about the then Serbian
province of Kosovo, the late former president Slobodan Milosevic suc-
cessfully managed to create this sentiment.[1] Milosevic depicted Kosovo as
a historical Serbian homeland allegedly taken over by ethnic Albanians
(Glenny 1992). In so doing, he sowed the seeds for his plan to cleanse
the province of Kosovo of ethnic Albanians a decade later.

Militarized Serbian nationalism has also been produced through and against Croatian nationalism, when Croatian leaders declared independence from the former country of Yugoslavia. Much of the territory claimed was home to Serbian people who found themselves an unwanted minority in the new Croatian nation. Following the secessionist moves of Serbia and Croatia and fearing minority status in a Serbian-dominated state, the state of Bosnia-Herzegovina formed in 1992, but not without considerable bloodshed produced by competing nationalisms. Bosnia-Herzegovina incorporated a more mixed set of ethnicities; Croats, Bosnian Muslims, and Serbs were all part of the final mapping of territory outlined in the 1995 Dayton Accord.

Few references are made to the significant proportion of mixed marriages in which the husband and wife came from different groups (Morokvasic-Müller 2004). Such families were often destroyed by nationalist fervor, which forced individuals to choose between their nation and their spouses. Many had to flee and find sanctuary in another country of refuge or risk accusations of betraying their nation. The destructive power of nationalism was most evident in Bosnia-Herzegovina, a fledgling state struggling for existence against the wishes of Belgrade and its meager remnants of the former Yugoslavia (Ò Tuathail 2006).

In Sri Lanka, national identities also make up the grammar of state politics. Nationalism has long incited fear among Tamil, Muslim, and Sinhala ethno-national groups. The framing of conflict from 1983 and 2009 has been portrayed primarily as a war between nations, Tamil and Sinhalese, though Sri Lankan Muslims have also been allies to both groups at different times in the conflict's history. School textbook representations of Sinhala rulers in relation to their Tamil opponents, for example, subscribe to a clear state-sponsored Sinhala nationalism as part of the national curriculum (Siriwardene et al. 1982). In a subsequent analysis of school texts, M. de Alwis (1998) challenges the "us-them" binaries behind these chauvinistic stories, but notes their importance in inculcating children with specific imaginaries of the hegemonic nation within the state. She demonstrates that tales of military vulnerability generate fear, followed by sentiments of courage and victory in the name of the nation. Sinhalese and Tamil nationalisms both became vehemently militarized and their conflict perceived as "ethnic" hatred, despite more subtle historical geographies and economies of marginalization, exclusion, and related vulnerability.

The quotidian geographies of fear experienced by minority national groups are largely invisible in places like Sri Lanka. A well-educated Tamil man who was born and raised in Colombo refuses to travel in motorized rickshaws, called three-wheelers, because of the exposure they represent to Sinhalese authority at security checkpoints. Another Tamil man who is married to a physician, also Tamil, discusses how he and his wife chose names for their children that were neither Tamil nor Sinhala so that they could "pass" in Badulla, the predominantly Sinhala town in which the family was based. Another well-educated Tamil couple, both with good jobs in Colombo though originally from Jaffna, decides to immigrate to Canada because prospects for their teenage children look so bleak. None of these stories gets written up as "research," but they represent subtle, everyday routines shaped by fear.

The production of nationalism in Sri Lanka is also linked to neoliberal economic changes. Before 1977 state socialism allowed the government to funnel funds to specific groups, making concessions especially to the Sinhalese rural middle and lower classes in order to be returned to power (Stokke 1998). After independence from Britain in 1948, political power was organized according to class more than national identity or ethnicity (Jayawardena 1990). Neoliberal economic policies signaled the end of the concessions that had held ethnic and class alliances together. While private investment began to flourish among some groups, Tamil majority areas in Sri Lanka's Northeast and Sinhala areas in the rural South remained largely excluded from this prosperity (Sivanandan 1990). In this context, economic marginalization produced fear and violent unrest among two groups excluded from the spoils of prosperity under the new neoliberal regime. The first comprised Sinhala youth from rural agricultural and middle classes who later formed the JVP, and the second was made up of a cadre of Sri Lankan Tamils who armed themselves against the government, namely the Tamil Tigers or LTTE (Gunasinghe 1987). Both groups used militarized nationalism and violence to advance their struggles.

Randomized violence that invokes public fear and kills unsuspecting civilians can be one response to feelings of exclusion and marginalization, especially if it is organized into nationalist projects. Such militarized violence characterizes the LTTE's bombing of public places and people during the mid- to late 1990s. In 2006, targeted attacks by the LTTE resumed; these acts are at once a response to violent expressions of Sinhala chauvinism against Tamils (such as government efforts to ethnically cleanse the capital city of Tamils on more than one occasion) and provocations in their own right. The Sri Lankan army and police have also been responsible for a host of abductions, deaths, and other human rights violations, especially in the Eastern Province, since the war began in 1983. These acts of violence have fueled oppositional nationalist movements on both sides of the majority Sinhala/minority Tamil divide. Militarized nationalism, whether Tamil or Sinhala, is about spatializing fear.

Under Siege: Home and Native Land

Alison Mountz (2003) and William Walters (2004) argue that security measures transcend the political borders of any single nation-state; instead they are organized increasingly on a transnational basis. Mountz shows how the state operates far beyond its territorial borders through airline carrier sanctions, offshore screening of passengers by airline liaison officers, and visa restrictions to exclude asylum seekers and other migrants. Walters introduces the complementary concept of "domopolitics" to suggest the central place of the home (domo) in geopolitical discourse:

> Domopolitics implies a reconfiguring of the relations between citizenship, state, and territory. At its heart is a fateful conjunction of home, land and security. It rationalizes a series of security measures in the name of a particular conception of home. . . . The home as hearth . . . as *our* place, where we belong naturally . . . home as a place we must protect. (2004, 241)

Home is a secure, reassuring place characterized by trust, togetherness, and familiarity. Home is a comfort zone and a fortress of sorts. A bifurcated sense of security is represented as both prosperity (economic) and risk (political). It requires different treatment of foreigners on the part of the state.

Neoliberalism normally refers to the deregulation of economies, the privatization of state assets, and accelerated integration into the global economy, whereas securitization points to the reregulation of borders, the strengthening of state enforcement resources and policies, and the rise of a more parochial domopolitics. Yet discourses of neoliberal globalization are not inconsistent with state discourses of securitization. They allow entry to skilled, elite migrants, but keep the suspicious, uninvited ones at bay—what Matt Sparke calls securitized nationalism. "By securitized nationalism I am referring to the cultural-political forces that lead to the imagining, surveilling and policing of the nation-state in especially exclusionary but economically discerning ways" (Sparke 2006, 153). The endangerment scenario of invasion is underwritten by securitization, a set of power relations based on mistrust and fear of the uninvited other (Bigo 2002).

The securitization of fear is a politically powerful resource for states that need legitimate grounds for extraordinary measures, such as violent exclusion from their territories. Yet "government practices of border control do not simply defend the 'inside' from the threats 'outside,' but continually reproduce our sense of the insiders and outsiders in the global political economy" (Amoore and de Goede 2005, 168). The securitized nationalism Sparke identifies produces a discursive distance and implied boundary between "us" and "them." This represents a deeply geographical problem that allows fear to be cultivated and to fester if left unchallenged. Both the competing nationalisms of Sri Lanka and the securitized nationalism of home are militarized geopolitical projects that spatialize fear in specific ways.

In the case of international aid, fear creates a crisis that foreign aid can be seen to fix. International aid becomes a tool for managing the risk of conflict, disease, and other threats spilling over into donor countries. Both aid and the buffer zones, to which I return at the end of the chapter, illustrate how fear is produced by and through specific political geographies of insecurity.

The Geopolitics of Conflict and Aid

Cultures of domination rely on the cultivation of fear as a way to ensure obedience. . . . As a culture we are obsessed with the notion of safety. (hooks 2000, 93)

It is a conviction of the times, this compulsion to hear how it [TV news] stands with the world, and be joined to the generality, to a community of anxiety. . . . A different scale of news value has been set by monstrous and spectacular scenes. (McEwan 2005, 176)

A "community of anxiety" is a potent resource, just as fear is a powerful emotion and tool mobilized to achieve various outcomes, political
and otherwise. The securitization of fear involves the rehearsal of loom-
ing threats and invasion. Speaking of the US role in Iraq, "The world's
most powerful military today is led by a cabal of restless nationalists im-
mersed in an anti-intellectual culture of affect and aggressive militarism"
(Ó Tuathail 2003, 857). Gearóid Ó Tuathail (aka Gerard Toal) reiterates
William Connelly's argument that human thought is not merely repre-
sentational but also "enactive" as affect (Connelly 2002).

Depending on context, concerns about survival, security, and sovereignty can be intimately linked to the production of fear at multiple
scales: of individual property owners, of minority national or ethnic
groups, of states that see themselves under siege. Fear is also used to set
in motion political demands for protection from often ill-defined, geographically diffuse threats: disease, asylum seekers, transnational crime,
terrorism—all ostensibly linked through a global web of risk. Individual
states may recognize shared insecurity and join forces on disease prevention, border protection, asylum policy, and intelligence related to
transnational criminal activity.

While immigration regulations and border controls are among the
most common sites of "securitization," foreign policy and development
aid have also become fertile ground for cultivating fear about the proliferation of conflict and its consequences in countries of the Global South.
The United States, Britain, Canada, and the Netherlands have integrated
development aid with foreign policy through this security discourse, coupling it with concern that aid be given where it can be most effective. Ultimately, these donor countries argue, aid effectiveness relies on political
stability, good governance (low levels of corruption being one indica-
tor), and neoliberal economic policies.

At the other end of the migration spectrum, fear of poor migrants
arriving uninvited and leaning too heavily on precarious welfare states is
a major concern for these same donor countries, particularly in Europe
where publicly funded services and infrastructure have historically been
more generous. Humanitarian assistance has become a de facto political
tool through which the threat to world stability and resources represented by poor countries may be defused by development (Canadian International Development Agency [CIDA] 2001).

On a more hopeful note, witnessing insecurity and disaster can instigate the political will to address the social and economic disparities that lead to conflict. Both the earthquake in Haiti and the 2004 tsunami evoked unexpectedly strong global responses that may have useful outcomes for the countries concerned. Disasters that create acute vulnerability and insecurity can also generate grounds for renewal. In their analysis of aid policy developments in Britain, David Slater and Morag Bell examine the Department for International Development's (DFID) 2000 White Paper: "There can be no secure future for any of us—wherever we live—unless we promote greater global social justice" (DFID in Slater and Bell 2002, 347). For the political constituency that once believed overseas development funds could be better spent at home, this trope denies and defies the geographical separation of "here" and "there," albeit in a politically retrograde manner. The "distinction between domestic and international policy is increasingly blurred" (ibid.). Foreign aid and development assistance to address material inequalities and political abuses are "for our own good," the well-being of donor societies.

In a similar if more fear-mongering vein, Canadian aid policy documents rehearse related tropes:

> Interdependence means that there is a convergence of interests among states around a wide array of issues—the environment, peace and security, health and the suppression of disease, economic and financial stability, migration and transnational crime. All states have interests in these issues—which can also have a strong values base—and advancing these interests requires, to a growing extent, improved international cooperation. (CIDA 2001, 4)

In short, "Canada's border is long and open to both commerce and people. Since disease does not need a visa, we cannot be healthy in an unhealthy world" (CIDA 2001, 6). Health and well-being at home demand international cooperation with other states. Foreign policy, including aid flows, can manage these geopolitical threats. Since aid policy in Canada became linked to security matters and foreign policy in 2000, development aid increased 8% every year to 2010. Relevant, effective aid programming is politically palatable to the governments that provide it.

The mobilization of fears that the "Third World" might leak into the "First World" has become a common, if not compelling, way to frame development assistance as foreign policy and as a security issue. Insecurity is expressed at different scales and from multiple perspectives: migrants, for example, at once fear the states at whose borders they arrive and yet embody insecurity in the imagination of those same states (Mountz 2010). Tacit geographies of "us" and "them" have emerged. Derek Gregory (2004, 28) asks, "How did those imaginative geographies solidify architectures of enmity that contrived to set people in some places against people in other places?" How are vulnerability and fear used to underwrite hate and violence?

The implications of these ties between aid and security usher in a distinct geographical imagination and constellation of politics. Increasingly, donor agencies align humanitarian and development assistance with issues of (in)security and (in)stability (Macrae and Leader 2000). Threats produce fear; fear can create a political willingness to act or acquiesce to laws, policies, and practices that might not otherwise be acceptable. This is the securitization of fear.

An often unstated role of development agencies is to manage risk associated with developing countries by (a) providing development aid where it will stabilize a developing country and increase its economic growth, or (b) withholding aid to "rogue" states until they come into line with donors' criteria for aid. By making development assistance conditional upon "good governance" in recipient countries, donors can indirectly address geopolitical threats. Donor states essentially establish their own political model as a prerequisite for the provision of assistance that is then used to address foreign policy concerns.[2]

Risk appears to be managed, on the one hand, through neoliberal policies of aid and trade that engender security and prosperity, and on the other, through policies of securitization built upon tropes of threat that inculcate fear. As Didier Bigo (2002, 63) has argued, "Expansion of what security is taken to include effectively results in a convergence between the meaning of international and internal security." Evoking fears of "over there" at home through a state-sponsored nationalism is politically persuasive. Fear and insecurity are linked across scales, from the bodies of migrants who represent insecurity in the imagination of states to the bifurcated transnational networks of biopolitical surveillance (Sparke 2006). Fear creates a crisis in search of a response.

Aid policy can use politically fertile threats of human invasion, un-invited disease, and transnational crime to create fear and consent for security measures that might not otherwise fly. On the upside, a belief that aid might stem migration instigated by conflict or environmental disaster by improving life for those affected at home legitimizes its flows.

The Sri Lankan Political Landscape

Moving to a less state-centric and geopolitical context, the conflict in Sri Lanka provides a vivid space in which nationalism, violence, and fear mixed in fatal ways. Two key moments of political geography begin to illustrate the relations of fear and mistrust among particular sectors of Sri Lankan society. First, on July 23, 1983, members of the LTTE ambushed an army patrol on the Jaffna Peninsula, a predominantly Tamil area, and killed 13 soldiers. Government troops in Jaffna took revenge in the hours that followed and killed 51 unarmed Tamil civilians (Swamy 1996). In Colombo the next day, the government decided to publish, broadcast, and televise news about 13 soldiers being killed by the LTTE while blacking out reprisals by the armed forces against Tamil civilians. By July 25, anti-Tamil violence spread throughout the city, enabled by the government's media presentation and by the police who largely stood by and witnessed the looting of Tamil businesses, murder of Tamil civilians, and widespread displacement of Tamil residents.

Later, in 1990, over 300 Muslims, men and boys, were prostrate in prayer at the Meera Jumma Mosque in Kattankudi along Sri Lanka's east coast when a power cut threw the mosque into darkness. LTTE cadres entered the mosque and opened fire; 140 men and boys were killed, most shot in the back. In Eravur, a town not far away, two weeks later another 173 Muslim men, women, and children were murdered in an effort to ethnically cleanse Muslims from Tiger-controlled territory. Many families fled to the Western Province of the country and established temporary homes in Puttalam District. Two decades later, they hold ration cards as proof of their displacement and entitlement to government support. Many still hold deeds and title to lands left behind in the early 1990s (Brun 2008).

In Sri Lanka the devastation of the tsunami and the aid that followed overlay longstanding geopolitical tensions and political geographies of displacement (Hyndman and de Alwis 2004). For example, many people displaced by the tsunami had already been displaced by war. Displacement has become a way of life for some Sri Lankans. Exacerbating this situation, many international NGOs that arrived on the scene in the immediate aftermath of the tsunami neglected to consult their national and local authorities, as well as their INGO counterparts (Couldrey and Morris 2005; Institute for Policy Studies 2005). Instead, INGOs competed for their slice of the humanitarian pie. The implementation of buffer zones in 2005 added a further layer of displacement. All in all, tsunami reconstruction in Sri Lanka has taken place alongside and in concert with rising political tensions among ethnic groups and with bitter bipartisan party politics. Aid workers in this environment have themselves become victims of violence. In 2006 an unprecedented attack on fifteen staff working for an international relief organization along Sri Lanka's east coast resulted in a mass murder (Apps 2006).

Nationalism, Conflict, and the
Case of the Buffer Zones

In January 2005 the Sri Lankan Cabinet of Ministers legislated no-build buffer zones along the coasts, ostensibly as a public safety measure against the potential devastation of another tsunami (Jansz 2005; Centre for Policy Alternatives 2005). As noted in Chapter 2, the densely populated Southern Province is dominated by people from the Sinhala majority and also host to most domestic and international tourism. Here, a one-hundred-meter buffer zone was established. However in the Tamil- and Muslim-dominated Eastern Province, where tsunami-related devastation had been greater, a two-hundred-meter buffer zone was declared.

At the time, the Opposition noted that Clause 14 of the Sri Lankan constitution guarantees people the right to live in areas of their choice. The Opposition said it would rescind the buffer zone requirement if elected to power, immediately politicizing the buffer zone policy (Tissera 2005). The buffer zones created contested political spaces characterized by polarized party politics, and an "opportunity to fish for votes" (K. de Alwis 2005). For example, because land within any buffer zone could still be used for business purposes, business owners appeared to be privileged over residential owners, benefitting the tourist operators in Sinhala-dominated beach areas of southern Sri Lanka (MONLAR and ANRHR 2005). Operators of beach hotels that were damaged but not destroyed by the tsunami could and quickly did restore their properties and continue business as usual whereas homeowners were forbidden to rebuild.

The "no build areas" policy may have been a genuine attempt to move people's residences away from the coast to prevent future deaths should another tsunami occur. However, no research, rationale, or evidence of how this approach would work was provided at the time of its introduction. The specific environmental, social, and physical characteristics of coastlines in different parts of the country require responses tailored to those geographies, but none was forthcoming. For those who had lost family members and homes, the prospect of losing their property and places of work as well (many were fishers) was extremely unwelcome. In June 2005 a poll of those displaced from these areas showed that 65% shunned the idea of the buffer zone (Kangararachchi and Range 2005). The apparent geographical "fix" of buffer zones served instead to fan the flames of political controversy between the major political parties and among the various ethno-national groups that constitute the Sri Lankan populace, namely Sinhala, Tamil, and Muslim groups.

The idea of buffer zones was co-opted by the Tamil insurgents as an expression of their own authority. In the North and Northeast, a four-hundred-meter buffer zone was declared by the LTTE. This was an assertion of its declared sovereignty in the area, known as the Wanni, that the rebels controlled (Jeyeraj 2005). The population in the Wanni was sparse in contrast to the heavily populated east coast and the densely settled South, so this huge no-go area was less controversial.

Until the end of the war, LTTE sovereignty was institutionalized in a number of interesting ways beyond the example of the buffer zones. The humanitarian arm of the LTTE, the Tamil Rehabilitation Organization (TRO), was one of the first agencies to build appropriate, well-lit transitional shelters in the Wanni after the tsunami hit. These temporary homes were well-planned and had decent, if basic, facilities for families displaced by the tsunami. LTTE did much more to distinguish this part of Sri Lanka from the rest of the country. A different time zone marked a separate state: thirty minutes different from the one used by the rest of the country. Where the LTTE claimed control, police and border officials all wore uniforms with the crest of "Tamil Eelam," the separate state that the Tigers sought. Foreigners had to show passports in order to enter, and letters outlining their work in the area were required. Many Sinhalese Sri Lankans could not easily gain access to this part of the Wanni at all.

After the tsunami, the buffer zones served to displace yet again those dispossessed by its waves and reproduced patterns of apparent discrimination against minority Tamils and Muslims. Many of those displaced by the tsunami in the hardest-hit eastern districts of Batticaloa and Ampara had already been displaced by the conflict, in some cases repeatedly, and had been living in makeshift seaside homes easily swept away by the tidal waves. Ironically the dramatic dispossession caused by the tsunami brought to light the endemic displacement of so many people who had been forced to move *to* these seaside locations to escape the war and seizure of territory by warring factions (Grundy-Warr and Sidaway 2006). The war, the tsunami, and the buffer zones each constitute a layer, or moment, of displacement for those in these two eastern districts.

While the initial conception of one-hundred-meter and two-hundred-meter buffer zones (and four hundred meters in LTTE-controlled areas) remained politically and scientifically suspect, the government of President Chandrika Kumaratunga adamantly maintained the policy for almost a year. As a concession to protests against the setback areas, the president did appoint a body of foreign experts to study the matter (Fernando 2005). Cracks in the government line on buffer zones began to show late in her presidency. In October 2005 the Advisory Council of the Coast Conservation Department began approving exemptions from the buffer zone policy (Cassim 2005). While most criticism of the buffer zones was homegrown (K. de Alwis 2005), some observers attribute the shift toward exemptions to former US president Clinton's assessment during a May 2005 visit to Sri Lanka that the buffer zones were impractical. As one journalist wrote, it "was after the Clinton remarks that the government woke up to reality" (A. Perera 2005).

In early 2005, with my Sri Lankan colleague and friend, Mala de Alwis, I was part of an UNICEF assessment that examined security in the temporary shelter encampments throughout the country. Along the east coast where fear for personal safety was greatest among residents, at least as far as we could glean, precarious communities of trust and relative peace before the tsunami had been replaced with new temporary formations of strangers living together in close proximity. The loss of familiarity, trust, and indigenous authority structures was witnessed in the exploitation of unaccompanied minors, and even the rare abduction of teenage girls by men who claimed to be their uncles.

Fear of another tsunami has also been used to legitimate buffer zones, and now conservation guidelines are being used as a more scientific marker of setbacks. The setbacks, both literal and figurative, have generated uncertainty and hopelessness regarding the reconstruction of permanent homes. Measures implemented in the name of public safety have had precisely the opposite effect, generating communal tensions, personal insecurity, and everyday fear among those in temporary accommodations in the Eastern Province.

Conclusion

Have his anxieties been making a fool of him? It's part of the new order, this narrowing of mental freedom, of his right to roam. . . . He suspects he's becoming a dupe, the willing, febrile consumer of news fodder, opinion, speculation and all of the crumbs the authorities let fall. He's a docile citizen watching Leviathan grow stronger while he creeps under its shadow for protection. (McEwan 2005, 180)

Fear serves many functions. It can be a basis for the "docile citizen" or an imperative for aid policy. It can even serve as the rationale for buffer zones in the wake of a tsunami. Threats of invasion—by refugees, disease, or transnational crime—are used to underwrite aid policy and flows. Insecurity and fear can drive aid politics in donor countries by producing a feeling of greater safety if aid is used to stabilize conflict and disaster elsewhere. This chapter has exposed some examples of geopolitical uses and abuses of fear in the context of disaster, conflict, and displacement. Both the ethno-nationalisms of Sri Lanka and the securitized nationalism of "home" in countries of the global North are geopolitical projects that spatialize fear in specific ways.

Just as fear creates grounds for suspicion, it needs to be treated, both intellectually and politically, with suspicion. Without constant vigilance that questions the existence of crisis and the fear it can engender, both of these commodities will be used creatively and strategically to justify violence and exclusion. Of course, fear may also help people survive, avoid risks, and build their homes farther from the sea. Yet, as an emotional response to threats, fear can forge adversarial mind-sets in both donor and recipient states that can lead to irrational and unjust behaviors. Likewise, fear can be unravelled, refused, or negotiated to subvert perceived threats, keeping projects like nationalism in check.

Where threats are debunked, fear can be transformed into hope and material spaces of solidarity, as politically astute groups of women from "enemy" nations came together to tackle ethnic chauvinism and rampant nationalism in young countries like Bosnia-Herzegovina (Cockburn 1998). Graffiti on the remnants of a water well destroyed by the tsunami reads, "Hope is life" (see Figure 3.1). Challenging the proliferation of fear by states, multilateral institutions, and militant nationalists is vital to changing a political climate of mistrust and geographical exclusion (Hyndman 2005b). Echoing the words of Nesiah, Nanthikesan, and Kadirgamar (2005) in Sri Lanka, "In honor of the dead then, let us make this moment of collective mourning also an opportunity to make a commitment to an ethos of pluralism, human security and democratization."

Figure 3.1 Graffiti on the Remnants of a Well Destroyed by the Tsunami Reads, "Hope Is Life"

The tsunami and its aftermath produced their own class fractions, cultural exclusions, and nationalist fears, none of which have disappeared with the official end of the conflict. And the buffer zones did nothing to allay such tensions. Climates of fear are, however, made, not given. Unraveling the ways in which fear is produced and framed to legitimate violence, provoke communal tension, and increase the discursive distance between "here" and "there" exposes grounds for hope.

Notes

1. While Kosovo is employed as the name of this now autonomous entity in international relations parlance, ethnic Albanians from this former province call it Kosova. The naming is obviously highly political.

2. Slater and Bell's (2002) postcolonial approach to analyzing development asks, "Who are the agents of knowledge, where are they located, for whom do they speak, how do they conceptualize, where are the analytical silences, who is being empowered, and who is being marginalized?" (339).

4

Transforming Widowhood: Conflict and Loss in Post-Tsunami Sri Lanka

Humanitarian aid, that which preserves life in the first instance, is meant to support survival through the provision of food, clean water, shelter, and basic medical assistance. Responses to environmental disasters tend then to be logistical affairs. Houses need rebuilding; wells must be drilled anew; schools and hospitals require reconstruction; bridges must be replaced and roads repaired. All of these activities were undertaken in Sri Lanka after the tsunami. During a complex emergency where two crises come together, however, ensuring people's survival and replacing infrastructure or livelihoods (see the broken boat in Figure 4.1) are the obvious responses. How such crises transform social relations and cultivate new survival strategies in the longer term is much harder to ascertain.

Many scars and losses were less visible to the naked eye, especially to the foreign eye. Social relations had also been destroyed or destabilized in the wake of a tsunami that left so many dead. Husbands lost wives; wives lost husbands; parents lost children; children lost parents and grandparents. . . . Some families were reduced to a single member. How were the survivors to cope with this loss and to rebuild their social networks? While some recognition of this struggle was evident in post-tsunami relief efforts, the understanding was inadequate. A plethora of psychosocial projects to address the loss of family members, home, and community were introduced before any clear assessment of actual trauma and need was conducted (M. de Alwis 2009). More than five years after the tsunami, several evaluations and assessments of the tsunami's impact

Figure 4.1 Broken Boat on Sri Lanka's East Coast, February 2005

and of the reconstruction efforts have taken place (TEC 2006), revealing new problems and gaps in the humanitarian response.

Gender roles and relations were reorganized by the tsunami in Sri Lanka, at least at the outset. A number of safety concerns emerged in early 2005 when I worked as a volunteer consultant with UNICEF in February 2005.[1] The Oxfam report of March of the same year has highlighted some of these issues:

> How safe are women in crowded camps and settlements, when they are so outnumbered by men . . . ? Will widows . . . have access to land once owned by their husbands? Will younger women enter into marriages with much older men. . . . In whose names will newly built houses be registered? Will men take on new domestic roles, or will women's workloads increase? (Oxfam International 2005, 2)

In this chapter I address some of these questions that have not received the same attention as issues of housing, livelihoods, and psychosocial rehabilitation. In particular, I focus on the issue of widowhood. How did the tsunami change the experience of home, family, and security for those who lost a spouse? Is remarriage an option? How have domestic roles changed? Interviews with forty widows and widowers along the east coast of Sri Lanka in February 2006 suggest that the tsunami not only reorganized gender relations among specific ethno-national groups, but also changed the meaning of "widow." Specifically, this study of widowhood in the towns of Batticaloa and Akkaraipattu begins to probe changes in the everyday geographies, power structures, and routines of people severely affected by the tsunami. I also examine the way in which war widows and tsunami widows are positioned differently within post-tsunami society and across ethnic groups.

Why Did So Many Women Die?

> Disasters, however "natural," are profoundly discriminatory. Wherever they hit, pre-existing structures and social conditions determine that some members of the community will be less affected while others will pay a higher price. (Oxfam International 2005, 1)

After the tsunami, Oxfam International (2005) conducted a multi-country study which reported that women were up to three times more likely to have died than men. The same ratio was reported by another source in Sri Lanka, where more than three times as many women as men died in the sixteen-to-thirty-year-old age group, leading experts to fear that the tsunami could have long-term detrimental effects on the birth rates in tsunami-affected regions (Sri Lankan Government and Development Partners 2005, 30).

Sarala Emmanuel (2005) conducted a post-tsunami study of two hundred households in Batticaloa that examined housing, livelihoods, human loss, and related issues identified by the people interviewed. From her sample, which was predominantly Tamil (93%), she found that 80% of the people who died in the tsunami were women and girls. Not only were female lives more likely to be lost, but women's wealth, often in the form of gold jewelry (but also bicycles), was also swept away by the destructive waves.

Certainly women were killed in greater numbers than men, a result that was as much socially produced through caregiver roles, socialization as children, and gendered clothing norms as due to any physical differences in strength. The skill sets of women and men are, for example, highly gendered. As Shanthi Sivasanan, Oxfam program assistant, reports, "Many men climbed trees to escape the water—it was something they had done many times before to pick fruit and while playing—yet women had never done this before and so didn't do it" (Oxfam International 2005).

In their study of the tsunami's impact on women in Batticaloa and Hikkaduwa, de Mel, and Ruwanpura (2006) explain that one reason so many women were killed was that many villages hold markets called *polas* on Sundays, the day the tsunami hit. These markets, or fairs, are generally located on the main coastal roads, not far from the seaside, where women buy and sell their produce. Women's labor thus positioned them in spaces of vulnerability in relation to the tsunami—marketing, washing pots and pans, and looking out for their children's safety. One woman recounts the day the tsunami hit, and how her clothing choice increased her mobility in relation to other women:

> I was at the fair when the waves came. . . . When I saw the wave I ran back, passed the railway tracks, and went to the station. I was wearing a maternity frock. I heard that women who were wearing tight skirts got caught to the wave and died as it was difficult for them to run.
> —Manel, a twenty-six-year-old woman from Seenigama.
> (cited in de Mel and Ruwanpura 2006, 21)

Gendered work situated women geographically near the seashore for marketing the day the tsunami hit. But as the theoretical framing outlined below illustrates, gender was not the only set of power relations at work that fateful day.

Framing Gender as Political: Feminism and Disaster

I make the case here for a robust and inclusive feminist approach to humanitarian disasters. Why a feminist approach and not a gender analysis? Analyzing gender disparities alone in the context of humanitarian crises, when power relations have gone awry, is insufficient. I employ the term "feminist" here in a broad sense to describe analyses and interventions that address the multiple differences and locations that generate inequalities and even violent relationships among people and places, including but not limited to gender relations. In Sri Lanka, the social impact of the 2004 tsunami cannot be divorced from the preexisting landscape with its layers of conflict, nationalism, and economic disparities. I argue that a "feminism and disaster" lens should be coupled with a "feminism and development" approach to understanding change in the wake of the tsunami. Focusing on gender relations alone is not enough.

War destabilizes gender and other social relations in ways that are often detrimental to women, but also enabling. On the one hand, conflict tends to create conditions that make women more susceptible to sexual assault or sex work. On the other, Tamil women in the north-central part of Sri Lanka controlled by the LTTE, the Wanni, were allowed to ride bicycles and travel alone to food markets once fuel for public transit in the northern parts of the country became scarce (Hyndman and de Alwis 2003). As the Oxfam quotation at the outset of the chapter implies, no disaster—whatever its antecedents—is gender neutral. Just as any disaster will discriminate by class, ethnicity, and location, gender matters, too (Hyndman and de Alwis 2003).

Joni Seager (2006) calls for researchers to pay attention to the ways in which disasters are gendered, but is a gender analysis alone sufficient? I contend that gendered relations are shaped not only by the tsunami but produced at the intersection of social, economic, and political relations and the ongoing conflict in Sri Lanka. These power relations are inseparable from one another. I make the case that academics and practitioners must both go beyond "gender and development" or "gender and disaster" frameworks to incorporate a fully feminist lens in analyzing conditions and responses to dispossession, destruction, and resulting impoverishment.

A feminist lens centers gender as a major axis of difference and disparity, but not the only nor necessarily the primary one. One's religious affiliation or minority/majority status in a particular location may be more important in shaping spaces of subordination than one's gender identity. A feminist approach examines how gender differences produce material, social, and other inequalities between the sexes, but also how other social locations (such as caste, class, and ethno-national identity) produce disparities and marginalization. Specifically, how do gendered identities such as "widow" vary across different ethnic groups—that is, Tamil, Sinhala, Muslim—and across circumstances of widowhood—

war widow or tsunami widow? Disasters put inequalities into stark relief. One aim, then, is to probe how responses to disasters can avoid reproducing inequalities.

Humanitarianism refers to programming and policies that relate to working in conflict or disaster zones where first and foremost the right to life is protected through the provision of basic necessities. Much of the aid programming in Sri Lanka, however, goes far beyond this minimum, blurring into full-scale development work. The importance of looking critically at both the longer-term development project and the emergency humanitarian one at the same time is vital, as these projects overlap. A brief overview of feminist literature on women in development and gender and development that informs humanitarian policy and practice today (Hyndman 1998) is necessary at this point.

WID, WAD, GAD, FAD: The Acronyms of Gender at Work

Examining gender relations in the context of humanitarian disasters is not sufficient (Hyndman and de Alwis 2004). Instead, I reiterate the case for a feminist approach that probes the very assumptions of development, livelihood, security, and assistance in contexts where power relations are never equitably distributed. How has development thinking in this realm morphed from a focus on "women" to "gender" to "feminist"?

The institutionalization of "women in development" (WID) in the early 1970s was largely a result of liberal feminist agitations globally. Women were added to the development project, much as women were added to the voters' list in liberal democracies, starting in the late nineteenth century. Charges that development was gender-blind or that it excluded women altogether were met with WID initiatives. While WID promoted integration into an existing masculinist (and Western) project of development, proponents of "woman and development" (WAD) considered such inclusion insufficient, and advocated separate projects for women and designed by women. Critics of WAD, however, questioned how two separate paths to development could be sustained, which would be funded, and whether disparate power relations between women and men were even addressed in the WAD approach.

The "gender and development" (GAD) approach was influenced by socialist feminist critiques of the modernization paradigm (including development), which emerged in the 1980s. Instead of focusing on women per se, the central concern of GAD approaches was the "social construction of gender and the assignment of specific roles, responsibilities, and expectations to women and to men" (Rathgeber 1990, 494). GAD began to examine power relations between men and women, as well as the gender identities associated with them. What, for example, does it mean to be a man in a particular historical, cultural, and geographical context? What does it mean to be a woman? How can development approaches engage such meanings rather than impose their own norms, and possibly create conflict or unwelcome change? In short, GAD approaches served to shift the focus away from "women" alone toward a much more comprehensive analysis.

The GAD approach questions the underlying social, economic, and political antecedents of uneven gender relations, and "demands a degree of commitment to structural change and power shifts that is unlikely to be found either in national or international agencies" (Rathgeber 1990, 495). This commitment to structural and relational change, however, is lost when researchers, governments, or agencies simply invoke the categories of women or gender in an effort to include gender programming in their projects. Every humanitarian project, in its design, method, evaluation, and impact, is gendered, just as it is embedded in culturally and politically specific frames of reference. In Sri Lanka, the fact that most income generation projects for women enable them to work from or near home (i.e., poultry rearing, home gardening) carries with it an implicit assumption that women are inextricably linked to the private, gendered sphere of the home, often through informal work such as caregiving, cooking, and cleaning.

Stereotyped roles in society can be perpetuated through the training of women in particular kinds of skills and professions. For example, NGOs with a mandate to restore livelihoods to women affected by humanitarian crisis are more likely to teach sewing and weaving—"feminine" skills—than masonry or carpentry (Hyndman and de Alwis 2003).

GAD begins to probe the implications of men and women as constructed identities, not as groups with internally coherent fixed roles or meanings. GAD also examines the power relations and division of labor between men and women, but I contend that it does not go far enough.

Instead of GAD, my colleague, Mala de Alwis, and I proposed FAD: feminism and development, which we take to include humanitarian efforts as well—hence, feminism and disasters as another definition of the acronym. FAD, either as feminism and development or feminism and disasters, is an enhanced analytical framework that incorporates multiple bases of identity such as ethno-national identity or caste, not exclusively gender. In the case of Sri Lanka, gender identity cannot be neatly separated from national identity. They are mutually constitutive. What it means to be a woman in Sri Lanka is shaped by one's religion, cultural heritage, mother tongue, caste, and history in a particular location (Ruwanpura and Humphries 2004; Ruwanpura 2006). In fact, one's mobility and employment opportunities during the Sri Lankan conflict were shaped as much by ethno-national affiliation as by gender.

By way of example, three young unmarried Muslim women living in Ampara District were not allowed to move around in public without a male relative escorting them. Their mobility was shaped by when and where these close relatives were available. The women were not allowed to work outside the home, but each was granted permission to attend an all-women class funded by a Canadian NGO, World University Service of Canada (WUSC). WUSC has been operating in Sri Lanka for more than two decades, in both the impoverished, conflict-affected eastern region, and in other Sinhala-majority areas. Attempts by WUSC along the east coast to offer co-ed classes in masonry, carpentry, welding, and tractor and bicycle repair, with a certain number of spaces reserved for women, largely failed.[2] The mixing of unmarried women with men was not popular with the families of the women, Tamil or Muslim. So women-only classes were run alongside the men's classes. Working with Mala de Alwis, we traced the path of these young Muslim women whom we heard about from WUSC. They had graduated from the welding class in 2000, but they found it difficult to apply their new trade because they could not work outside the home and maintain their reputations. Yet innovation by the father of one of the women made employment for these women possible. He had a workshop built for welding that was attached to, and thus considered an extension of, the family home (see Figures 4.2 and 4.3).

This spatial innovation was admittedly exceptional, but the story shows that WUSC was bending gender norms by training women in these occupations, and that women and their families were finding ways to bend social norms in order to make work possible. In this case, Muslim norms about women's mobility in public space were subverted by extending private space to include a workshop.

Figure 4.2 Extending Workspace in a Muslim Home, Ampara District, Sri Lanka

Figure 4.3 Woman Welding "At Home," Ampara District

Gender and Nation

Gender relations are part and parcel of nationalist discourses (Jayawardena 1986), but also of class, caste, colonialism, religion, language ability, and location (Elliott 2005; Bagwe 1998). Nationalism may seek to homogenize differences under the unifying discourse of the nation, but it also generates contradictory positions for women as symbols of cultural purity, agents of resistance against Western domination, and subjects of the nationalist patriarchal family (Hyndman 2005a). National identity is not a fixed notion, nor can it claim a unitary subject separate from gender, race, caste, class, and religious identity. National identity thus intersects with gender relations and racism in particular permutations and combinations. Nationalist projects demand attention because of the ways in which they construct and claim men and women as part of the nation, and because of the ways in which belonging is used as a basis for killing women and men of other nations (Yuval-Davis 1998).

Men, too, are cast in specific roles in relation to the nation. Men are generally expected to defend the integrity of the nation and its territory, which generally includes the reputation of "their" women. Being a man connotes certain social roles in a context where nationalism and militarization intersect: men tend to be seen as the principal combatants and can therefore be the first targets in campaigns to eliminate or force out a particular ethnic/national group. A feminist approach that incorporates historicized and geographically situated identities, including gender, is a more compelling position from which to transform relations that provoke or perpetuate violence, hate, and inequality.

My use of feminist thought is deliberate, if provocative to some. To assume that gender is somehow the primary category of analysis or the most disparate axis of difference within a context of neoliberal imperatives, competing nationalisms, and other prejudices is too simplistic. As Chandra Mohanty (2003) argues, the category of "woman" is inherently unstable. That is to say, the internal coherence of the category is low. The people who belong to the category "women" may have little in common with one another beyond gender identity. Women, or men, who have been displaced from their homes because they are from a minority ethnic group in a region of the global South have little in common with those who live in peaceful and prosperous states of the global North.

Meaning varies across ethno-national identity and geographic location, as well as by gender.

Ultimately, these various affinities and differences overlap and intersect in ways that position people very specifically in relation to each other. While GAD approaches do commit to structural and relational change where necessary, they assume that change will need to be made in relation to gender. Caste bigotry, ethno-national differences, and the economic geographies of displacement due to war are not taken into account by GAD. For example, the area of Sri Lanka most affected by war is also the area most adversely affected by the tsunami. The Eastern Province is also disproportionately populated by two minority ethnic groups, Tamils and Muslims. The empirical section of this chapter, then, aims to show that the very meaning of 'widow' in this region is unstable in the context of ethno-national identity, war, and disaster.

I elaborate below first on the unstable meaning of "widow" in eastern Sri Lanka, given the differences that ethnicity makes, and second on the insecurities both widows and widowers face since the tsunami.

Destabilizing the Categories "Women" and "Widow": Gender Meets Nation

Gill Valentine (2007) analyzes intersectionality in feminist scholarship, arguing that not only are identities co-constituted across multiple axes of difference (including but not limited to gender) but also that different identities may come to the fore at different times. Valentine uses the metaphor of "geometries of oppression" to trace how identity is done, by whom, and when. "The identity of particular spaces—the home, the school, the workplace, or a community space . . . are in turn produced and stabilized through the repetition of the intersectional identities of the dominant groups that occupy them" (Valentine 2007, 19).

The foregrounding of particular identities can vary across a single lifetime. With respect to Sri Lankan widows, for example, Ruwanpura and Humphries (2004, 187) posit that a young widow with children is likely to face greater financial responsibilities than an older one with grown children: "The needs of a young widow with several dependent children whose husband has been killed in ethnic violence may be very different from the needs of a middle-aged widow with several children old enough to work." Furthermore, widows are cast as more deserving female heads of households than their non-widow counterparts. These authors question homogenizing accounts of Sri Lankan women's lives and explore ethnicity as a source that produces difference among woman-headed households in eastern Sri Lanka.

Significant differences exist across women-headed households despite "oppressive gender standards within both Sinhala and Tamil ethnic groups . . . emphasizing motherhood and sacrifice as the archetypal feminine path" (Ruwanpura and Humphries 2004, 179). Malathi de Alwis (1998) has written extensively about "moral motherhood" in the context of the war in Sri Lanka, and the ways in which women are used in nationalist projects as reproducers of the nation and bearers of cultural identity. Gender and ethnicity (or national identity), then, co-constitute and differentiate the meaning of "woman," and by definition "widow," in Sri Lanka.

Ruwanpura and Humphries (2004) also analyze factors that precipitate and inhibit woman-headed household formation, exposing significant differences among Tamil, Muslim, and Sinhala women, both widows and non-widows.[3] Where Sinhala women head of households stand to benefit from the Sinhalese legal code (including bilateral property inheritance laws) and their majority ethnic group status, Muslim women are hampered by restrictions on their mobility and related obstacles to income-earning opportunities (McGilvray 1982, 1989).

Distinct patterns of employment among Muslim, Tamil, and Sinhala women heads of household were noted, with 59.4% of Sinhala women participating in wage labor, compared to 17.2% for Tamil women and 31% for Muslim women with the same household configuration. Likewise, Sinhala women who were heads of household were less likely to be self-employed (23.3%) in relation to Tamil women (46.6%) and Muslim women (41.6%) in the Eastern Province where the study was conducted. The intersection of gender, ethnicity, and relations of paid work varied significantly across the various permutations of identity. "Woman" is, indeed, an unstable category.

More specifically, the rate of widowhood in the three districts surveyed well before the tsunami varied significantly by ethno-national identity. Whereas 52.2% of Sinhala women heads interviewed were widows, 67.2% of Tamil women and 61% of Muslim women heads were.[4] How these women were widowed was also probed in the study, revealing that

28% of Sinhala widows' husbands were killed (as opposed to dying of natural causes or disease) compared to 22% for Muslim women in the same position and 72% for Tamil women (Ruwanpura and Humphries 2004, 186). These differences are startling and point to the differential effect of the conflict on the households, as this study was conducted before the tsunami. In post-tsunami Sri Lanka, these figures have changed, as has the very meaning of "widow."

Tsunami Widows: Living With Insecurity

Post-tsunami Sri Lanka is not an easy place for single and widowed women. One major concern facing all widows as well as other survivors is security. At the time of the study, everyone we spoke to was living in transitional, or temporary, housing. A series of displacements from conflict, tsunami, and then buffer zones meant that many people, including those along the east coast interviewed for this study, had to live in temporary shelters at different locations from their original homes. Most Tamil and Muslim villages scattered along the coast in the Eastern Province were ethnically homogeneous to a significant extent before the tsunami. These precarious political geographies of separation, borne out of mistrust produced by the conflict, were drastically undone by the tsunami and the policy of buffer zones that led to a shortage of land on which to settle those displaced. New livelihoods were reestablished in temporary communities until land could be identified for more permanent housing (Centre for Policy Alternatives 2005).

The day of the tsunami, Manel and others mistook the event for a rebel attack:

> On the day the tsunami happened I was at the Sunday fair. People were crying that the LTTE was attacking. The noise of the wave crashing against the shops and buildings must have been so loud that everyone thought the Tigers were bombing the area. I thought I lost my child and my mother-in-law in the bombing. (cited in de Mel and Ruwanpura 2006, 24)

The landscape and legacies of the conflict are evident here. Fear of the war led to a misinterpretation of the sound of waves.

After the tsunami, other fears emerged. Camp life creates intense insecurity for certain segments of the Sri Lankan society, particularly unmarried women. One teenage girl, Mutur, explains the situation in which she finds herself:

> We are still living in a camp. My parents are trying to marry me off to a man who is 15 years older. They say they can't protect me, or give me dowry. I want to go back to school, study and then get a job. (Women and Media Collective 2005)

Widows also find themselves in an insecure position. Normally, widows who live without the protection of their extended family are harassed; their movements are judged suspiciously, and their reputations are always at stake. Prospects for subsequent marriages are slim (Bagwe 1998). The despair of one woman who was widowed by the conflict captures her precarious social and personal positioning; Jayanti says, "I had hope and happiness when my husband was alive. Now I have no hope. I have only fear and sadness. It's affecting my mind. [I'm] scared to keep my son. . . . What a life? [I] have to live in eternal fear."[5] Societal interventions to change public attitudes are necessary, as Deepa Mehta's provocative 2005 film *Water* illustrates, but the general insecurity of widows and of single women living alone has been a pressing issue for some time (de Alwis and Hyndman 2003).

The tsunami wiped out a whole set of social relations for some women, who lost not only their spouses but their own extended family and that of their dead husbands. Where they exist, these familial networks normally provide material support, social respectability, and security for widows. In their absence, social authority is destabilized. Says Vijaylakshmi, a twenty-five-year-old widow who lost her husband and three children in the tsunami,

> Before the tsunami I had my husband's protection. Now I live with my old mother. Brothers are not living near. So there is no protection.

Security is highly geographical, based on the proximity of male relatives. Yet it is also social. As Noor, a young widower, explained of the women who lost their spouses in the tsunami,

> The [women] widowed due to tsunami do not have anyone. No children, siblings, or parents. They don't have any protection or help. So they remarried to get some kind of comfort. Widows of war did not

lose all their relatives; so they did not want to remarry. (a twenty-one-year-old widower; no children)

From this young man's perspective, a woman who is widowed is without protection. Security is secured through social relations, especially marriage. Jeevan remarks,

> If a widow speaks to a male immediately they [the males] spread stories. This is why marriage takes place. There is no help for tsunami widows. No one to guide them. So if they decide, they remarry. During war, widows did not lose [all] their relatives. So they did not have any interest in remarrying. (a thirty-year-old widower, two small kids)

This excerpt explains that remarriage is a widow's choice, but is it a choice if she is without protection and perhaps material support and at risk of losing her reputation?

Vasuki, a twenty-eight-year-old woman who lost her husband, mother, two elder sisters, and a niece in the tsunami, laments the loneliness she experiences: "I live alone. . . . Housework has reduced. . . . Now loneliness is biggest torture." She notes that she would need US$2,000 as a dowry to remarry, and while she is unsure she wants to do so, remarriage is not simply her choice. A third man, Neelan, who lost his wife, echoes this idea that women choose, but also makes the key distinction between war widows and tsunami widows:

> The widows of tsunami lost everything in one day. They lost their relatives and have no protection or support. There is no one to comfort or to tell what is good or bad. Therefore they have remarried immediately. The final decision to remarry lies in their hands alone. But war widows had the support of their relations. (a forty-two-year-old widower who lost two children; one daughter survived)

According to these men, remarriage is purely practical, a necessity in the face of insecurity. They do not question why women are unprotected if they are outside marriage, nor suggest alternatives beyond marriage.

Women's own views on remarriage, at least those of the widows interviewed in this study, are distinct from the men's and complicated by concerns for their children's well-being. Radhika, a thirty-four-year-old widow with five surviving children, spoke firmly:

Women will not remarry. The man will definitely torture her children. Even during the war when women became widows they did not re-marry. My husband was very loving. I will not remarry. I think my trouble will be over when my eldest son completes his studies.

She observes that she will eventually have protection through her son, once he is old enough and has completed school. More important, the risk of having one's children mistreated by a new spouse seems to be a very vivid fear for more than just this woman. A forty-year-old widow named Sharada whom we interviewed also used the word "torture": "No woman known to me has remarried. Reason for this is that the new hus-band might torture the surviving children." Three more widowed women echo this sentiment:

> Most men have remarried. Very few women have married. *Most of the men (except three) have got married to young women.* I feel that people with children should not remarry. They'll be step-parents and chil-dren will get affected by this. (Aananthi, age thirty-seven, with two surviving children, ten and seven; italics added)
>
> I'm not interested in remarriage. There'll be problems. (Mala, age twenty-five, who lost her husband and three children)
>
> Very few women have remarried. Men normally get [re]married. About ten marriages took place this week [of February 5, 2006]. So many marriages have taken place within the first month of Tsunami. *Most men have married young women.* Women are the ones who died more in the Tsunami, so more widowers than widows. (Waani, a forty-five-year-old woman who lost her two daughters, husband, and grand-children; one son [sick] survived; italics added)

Very clear concerns about the treatment of children by new spouses are voiced here. According to two women informants, widowers have been more likely to marry younger women (i.e., unmarried) where possible. The families of younger, not-yet-married women, who did not lose all their assets in the tsunami, are more likely to be able to provide a dowry for the daughter, making her more marriageable. As Vithy, a widow of forty-nine, stated,

> Very few women [get remarried]. But more men have married. *Fear is the main reason for women.* Also who has the ability to give dowry and get married? Men go outside their families and get married. (italics added)

Women's "choice," where a dowry is expected, is less about independent decisions and more about societal expectations that may have changed since the tsunami, but cannot be ignored altogether. Fear is also a driving force. Acute social stigma and economic insecurity are powerful forces in the post-tsunami context. The prospect of marriage or remarriage for single or widowed women in rural Sri Lanka is fraught, yet it has become more appealing as a way to mitigate insecurity than it was in pre-tsunami times.

We spoke to many men who lost their spouses and wanted to remarry. They saw marriage unproblematically as a "gender accessory." The idea that the tsunami reorganized the gender division of labor, especially the unpaid labor of childcare in the home, has been short-lived. Some of the men we interviewed did recognize childcare as hard work:

> The six months I spent looking after my children is the most difficult time. I don't know how women do all this work. I had to really struggle. (Lalith, a thirty-nine-year-old widower with three surviving children, now remarried with his new wife's two children)
>
> I am happy from the time I got [re]married. My new wife looks after me and my children the same way my first wife did. She washes my children's clothes. She protects us. (Paraj, a thirty-eight-year-old widower, with three surviving children who has remarried a thirty-five-year-old war widow with two children of her own)
>
> I have a son aged two and a half years. There is no one to look after him. . . . All what Chandra [his dead wife] did is done by me now. When I go to work I take him along to the work place. . . . I have plans to remarry. . . . You need another person's help, isn't it? (Danesh, a forty-eight-year-old widower)

Two of these men have happily remarried, and point to the unpaid domestic work that their new wives do for them. The third plans on marrying, for the help a wife would provide, he says. A slightly older man, Dano, who lost his wife and has three older children, is more reluctant to remarry:

> A man or women with a small child has to get married . . . [but] I think whoever gets married and comes won't look after like their own children. (a forty-two-year-old widower with two adult sons and one twelve-year-old daughter; he won't remarry, has to focus on marrying his kids)

Like the women above, he does not believe that his new spouse will necessarily treat his children properly. Another man speaks of the strife his plans for remarriage have caused. None of his family supports this decision:

> I have not remarried yet. I have spoken about it. She is a widow aged thirty-five years with two children. My sister-in-laws don't like the idea of me getting married to her. But I have decided. I am remarrying because I want my life to return to what it was like before. I need someone to cook and wash for me. . . . No one talks to me since I decided to get [re]married (my mother, my sister-in-laws). . . . Now I live a lonely life. (Kabil, a thirty-nine-year-old father of a thirteen-year-old girl)

Given the testimony about "torture" of two women above, it could be the well-being of the teenaged girl that concerns the extended family, though one cannot know this from the transcripts. In any case, remarriage for men appears to be a less fraught process than for women. Yet the absence of protection or security socially speaking appears to be a major consideration for widows or single women who find themselves without the presence of extended family.

When asked about their security, men interpreted the questions we asked quite differently:

> [We have] no protection. Earlier when we went to work, we did not have any problems on the way. No army or police checking. Now when we say we are from "Thirai madu" they think we are with the terrorists. Because of this there is more problems. We have to show proof with our identity cards. Once when they rounded us up, they made us kneel. (Babu, a twenty-one-year-old widower)
> There is more fear for safety now. (Faruq, a twenty-eight-year-old widower)
> There is no protection for our life (Rahul, a widower, forty-eight years old)

In these excerpts pertaining to security, all of the respondents refer to physical safety and the rise of insecurity in relation to daily mobility, not social insecurity.

Where the loss of family members from the tsunami has left women alone, widows find themselves in new situations of vulnerability. Just as "woman" is a precarious category that varies across national identity (i.e., ethnicity) or caste, "widow" is also a changing concept that has evolved since the tsunami.

Conclusion

This chapter has shown how "widow" and "women" are unstable categories in the context of war and tsunami. Both vary by ethnicity and by the kind of disaster that precipitated it. One's gender and ethnic identity, among other factors, co-constitute the meaning of "widow," but location in the conflict- and tsunami-affected areas also defines one's sense of self and security in a war zone. The meaning of "widow" is itself highly spatialized, shaped by successive waves of displacement from twenty-five years of conflict, from the tsunami in 2004, and from dislocation vis-à-vis the government's buffer zone policy since 2005.

Class, race, caste, sexuality, religion, nationality, and ethnicity are all potential bases for exclusion, discrimination, and even violence. As Gill Valentine (2007) argues, these strands of history and geography are not additive or separable from one another. Rather, a feminist approach that draws on intersectionality, like FAD, improves upon prevailing approaches to gender-based programming in NGOs, UN agencies, and donor circles. As an academic or a practitioner, one must focus not only on the differences between men and women after the tsunami, but on the differences within the categories "woman" and "man," "widow" and "widower."

A gender analysis alone is insufficient. The practices of aid, policy, and history that position certain groups of people in hierarchical relation to others are not easily unraveled, but a feminism and development approach coupled with a feminism and disaster approach can do this work. The well-intentioned work of development staff and humanitarian actors can unwittingly reproduce and perpetuate existing gender, racial, and geographical hierarchies by uncritically promoting certain kinds of projects—for example, sewing for poor, conflict-affected women (de Alwis and Hyndman 2002).

In relation to this study, my aim has been modest: I have probed the tsunami's impact on the meaning of "widow," the spaces and predicaments that widowers and widows occupy in post-tsunami Sri Lanka, and the ways in which households have been reconfigured. I wondered if the study might find some man-headed households with fathers cooking, cleaning, and looking after their children after the loss of spouses and mothers. An Oxfam officer in Akkaraipattu told me she knew of two men who were doing this work in February 2006, some fourteen months after the tsunami. They both, however, planned to remarry. The gender division of labor has not significantly changed. Women's workloads in some extended households have increased, but there is just as much evidence to suggest that women widowed by the tsunami have experienced a decrease in their workload, especially among those who lost children.

The men interviewed in Batticaloa and Akkaraipattu distinguished between war widows and tsunami widows, with the latter having less family protection and therefore more proclivity, in their minds, to remarry. They see remarriage as a decision or choice women make, despite the testimony from five women that they would not consider remarriage because it could be detrimental to their children's welfare. While legally outlawed, dowries still exist and also represent a major obstacle that widows face if they do, in fact, desire to remarry. For widowers with small children, in contrast, remarriage is seen as a necessity, as it is expected that a woman is needed to care for children, wash the family's clothes, and cook for the family in the long term.

With respect to two of the questions Oxfam posed in its March 2005 assessment of the tsunami—"Will younger women enter into marriages with much older men. . . . Will men take on new domestic roles, or will women's workloads increase?" (Oxfam International 2005, 2)—the answers appear, at least provisionally, to be yes, men are more likely to marry younger, unmarried women, though several have unexpectedly remarried widows of the tsunami and of war. The demographic implications of this shift in marriage patterns for younger unmarried men remains to be seen. Finally, men have not taken on new domestic roles permanently, in the face of losing their spouses.

On a more hopeful note, this study raises many more questions for further research. As de Mel and Ruwanpura (2006, 18) note, "Sri Lanka's property rights regime has been upheld as a feminist haven for its bilateral and matrilineal inheritance patterns through customary and codified law." Most of the people interviewed told similar stories: land titles were in the names of wives and daughters, though none had a new home yet due to the buffer zone policy. Given that the majority of new permanent homes have yet to be built (Centre for Policy Alternatives 2005), research on these issues will be needed once they have been built. Did women lose ground on property ownership, and if so, who did and why? Are there any patterns that suggest those of a specific ethno-national group, class, location, or gender lost out? More research on dual disasters, their impact on households and security, is sorely needed. This study scratches the surface; the longer-term social implications of the tsunami for families who lost so much remains to be done.

Notes

1. I was merely an assistant to my friend and colleague, Mala de Alwis, who was working as a genuine consultant for UNICEF at the time; nonetheless, we spent more than two weeks crisscrossing the country, talking with both conflict-displaced and tsunami-displaced people. I am grateful to Mala for including me in her work.

2. Overall, however, these programs are a good example of conflict-sensitive programming in that they provided skills development with funds that could not be diverted for other purposes.

3. The authors base their analysis on 298 interviews with women-headed households in the Trincomalee, Batticaloa, and Amparai districts of eastern Sri Lanka.

4. The authors note that the sample is not technically representative of all female-headed households but its size (298 interviews) suggests strong correlations nonetheless.

5. All names used are pseudonyms.

5

Acts of Aid:
Humanitarianism Meets
Neoliberalism in a War Zone

began research for this chapter in 2002 during a summer of meetings and interviews in Ottawa and Colombo. How, I wondered, would the neoliberal policy of aid effectiveness that had come into vogue play out at the CIDA? And specifically what would such a policy look like in practice on the ground in South Asian countries affected by conflict? The prerequisites for assistance under aid effectiveness include good governance and sound economic policies, yet by definition these seemed to exclude countries facing political instability, namely Sri Lanka, Nepal, and India.

This chapter analyzes the intersection of neoliberal development policies and post-tsunami aid specifically in Sri Lanka. Since 1977 Sri Lanka has lived with neoliberal policies of international assistance, and since 1983 it has been subject to a vicious war between government troops and militant rebels, the LTTE. International aid has focused on economic development and support for peace negotiations, but little attention has been paid to the ways in which neoliberal aid agendas intersect with conditions of conflict and insecurity to shape donor behavior and aid delivery. Drawing from primary research with bilateral aid agencies operating in Sri Lanka, particularly the CIDA, intersections between neoliberal development policies and negotiations for peace are probed in the context of international aid.

Introducing "Aid Effectiveness"

Identified first by Organization for the Economic Cooperation and Development (OECD 1992) and promoted by the World Bank (1998), "strengthening aid effectiveness" is a salient neoliberal policy of development that aims to utilize international assistance most efficiently by eliminating from the recipient list countries with protectionist economic policies or corrupt, unstable governments. Good governance and sound economic policy are prerequisites for receiving international aid under this policy rubric. Donors aim to consolidate their aid "investments" in countries where their "return" will be greatest in terms of "pro-poor growth" (Burnside and Dollar 1997). The neoclassical economic logic may be simplistic, but has proven politically persuasive to governments allocating funds to their aid agencies (Knockaert 2004). In fact, international aid budgets have increased where countries have adopted such policies (Sallot 2005). Aid effectiveness policies are politically persuasive in raising funds at home, and are tacitly about increasing the geopolitical influence of the donor nations (Munro 2005). In short, the allocation of much development aid is being reconfigured both geographically and programmatically.

The neoliberal policy of aid effectiveness overlaps with longstanding geopolitical priorities related to promoting security, democracy, and liberal, rights-based peace (Duffield 2008). During the Cold War, foreign aid to developing countries was as much about forging geopolitical allies and proving the superiority of capitalist economies as it was about remedying the "underdevelopment" of non-aligned Third World nations. The geopolitical aims of state security remain in place today, even if the threats to it have changed. Threats to national security, in particular, have stoked a geopolitics of fear that uses the threat of less developed countries invading or infecting donor countries if adequate aid transfers are not provided. The securitization of aid—that is, the tying of aid provision to the security agendas of the global North—is not particularly new (Duffield 2001) and is geographically widespread among donor countries (Macrae and Leader 2000; Bastian 2007b). The global North attempts, quite unsuccessfully, to isolate itself from the global South by exerting control over migration and security matters through a series of shared tactics (Amoore 2006; Mountz 2007).

Just as aid is subject to neoliberal norms, it has long been seen as a potential panacea and geographical fix for the disease, poverty, conflict, transnational crime, and uninvited migration from the global South that affects industrialized countries of the North (Duffield 2008). Aid is thought to be one tool for containing if not eliminating these social ills, as discussed in Chapter 3. Mountz (2003), Walters (2004), Sparke (2006), and Amoore (2006) illustrate how states produce a threat of a crisis—for example, uninvited migration from developing countries, to authorize various enforcement measures to eliminate the threat. Fear of invasion is a potent political resource, used to argue for increased aid budgets to combat insecurity. In theory, aid to promote development in poorer countries should contain the migratory effects of underdevelopment and keep the global North more secure (Duffield 2008).

Disaggregating aid into actual donors—mostly multilateral banks and bilateral agencies—that behave in very different ways is a related goal, demonstrating differences not only among donors but across distinct historical moments during which neoliberal aid, nationalism, conflict, and ceasefires combine in different permutations and combinations. By grounding these often ill-defined, aspatial, and free-floating concepts in the contentious political landscape of Sri Lanka, this chapter provides a closer reading of both the political reality of aid effectiveness effort and the incentives provided by international aid to broker peace.

The Case of Sri Lanka

Foreign aid now seems to be concerned with the total transformation of Sri Lankan society. (Bastian 2007b, i)

Sri Lanka was a country at war for more than twenty-five years and had been characterized by political unease for at least twenty-five years before that. Long before the 1983 pogroms that commonly denote the commencement of the war, the government's introduction of the 1956 Sinhala Only Act stirred up communal antagonism and generated considerable resentment among Sri Lankan Tamils (Gunasinghe 1987). This act declared Sinhala to be the only official language, removing Tamil as one of the state-sanctioned languages, and marking the Sinhala-led government as ardently nationalist. The constitution was eventually changed to make Buddhism Sri Lanka's "foremost" religion despite the presence of long-standing Hindu and Muslim communities. During this same period, Sri Lanka remained at the vanguard of the Non-Aligned Movement (NAM), avoiding allegiance with superpowers and practicing import substitution industrialization as far as possible (Sivanandan 1990). In desperate financial straits by the mid-1970s, the government reluctantly accepted international aid in the form of International Monetary Fund (IMF) loans. Not long after the arrival of neoliberal policies of structural adjustment, uprisings and armed conflict commenced.

I contend that a few key moments are illustrative of the recursive effects of war on international aid and of aid on conflict. First, the aforementioned IMF loans and official development assistance (ODA) to Sri Lanka in 1977 generated tensions in the country that were correlated with violence by two groups who felt disenfranchised by the changes they created. Second, the late 1980s were brutal years for human rights violations, both by government troops and rebels. The proliferation of abduction, torture, and disappearances sent tens of thousands of Sri Lankans, mostly Tamils, to seek refuge in other countries and displaced many more within the country's borders.[1] These atrocities forced donors to reconsider their bilateral aid allocations to a government complicit in such egregious violations. Third, the period from 2001 to 2004 is notable for a number of reasons. In 2001, for the first time since Sri Lankan independence in 1948, the country experienced negative economic growth after the LTTE blew up several commercial and military aircraft at Katunayake where a military airstrip and Bandaranaike International Airport are located. Later than same year, grounds for a ceasefire were laid and a plan for reviving the economy quickly put in place, yet 683,000 people were officially listed as internally displaced at that time (Muggah 2008). In February 2002 the ceasefire agreement (CFA) was signed between the government of Sri Lanka and the rebel LTTE, monitored by the Norwegian-led SLMM. Economic growth was restored quickly, but peace proved more elusive.

More than 680,000 Sri Lankans were internally displaced at the time the ceasefire was signed, with almost 175,000 living in welfare centers or relocation villages (Muggah 2008). This period of relative calm ushered in what has become loosely known as the "fifth peace process" (Stokke 2006), during which negotiations between the government of Sri Lanka and the LTTE continued.[2] The final moment is the 2004 tsunami, by which time peace negotiations between the LTTE and government of Sri Lanka had fallen apart. This context of failure and mistrust shaped government–rebel talks about humanitarian aid distribution across the country. Each of these moments embodies a key connection between the terms of aid and those of war.

Mapping out differences between international financial institutions (IFIs), concerned principally with promoting open markets and economic growth, and other donors more interested in peace-building projects and human rights disaggregates any simplified claim about foreign aid as singular or unified. Furthermore, international donors and the Sri Lankan state cannot be viewed as fully autonomous actors, whether pitted against one another or allied in their aims. Rather, they are in combination all vital brokers of social and economic development as well as of peace negotiations in Sri Lanka (Bastian 2007a). Tracing connections between international donors' wishes and those of a precarious democratic Parliament in Sri Lanka reveals the difficult dilemmas and political compromises that take place. In 2006 total foreign aid disbursements to Sri Lanka, a country of fewer than 20 million people, amounted to over $1 billion (ibid.).[3] The stakes are high.

In what follows, I start by critically engaging the assumptions of aid effectiveness policy. Second, I probe the securitization of aid and situate development assistance within these twin frames. I then move to the key moments of the development–security nexus identified above that demonstrate the impact of security and peace considerations on neoliberal aid, and vice versa. I conclude with a brief analysis of the 2004 tsunami, a disaster that devastated the country, but also created unique constellations of aid distribution. The role of nature in creating conditions of disaster and the political influence of the Sri Lankan Tamil diaspora point to geographies of hybridity and transnationalism that prove potent forces in shaping aid beyond the binary of aid effectiveness and security.

Primary research probing the actions of one aid agency operating in Sri Lanka, the CIDA, and secondary sources analyzing political negotiations and donor priorities are both used to generate an account of the intersection of neoliberal aid policies and security agendas in the Sri Lanka context.[4]

Neoliberal Aid: Strengthening Aid Effectiveness

In theory, "strengthening aid effectiveness" aims to reward low-income developing countries that demonstrate sound (i.e., competitive, open-market) economic provisions and good governance (i.e., stability and low levels of corruption) by selecting them for significant aid injections (CIDA 2001). But aid effectiveness is arguably just as much about remaining relevant as public policy and maintaining budgets at home as it is about development elsewhere. Dramatic budget cuts between 1990 and 1995 saw a decline in CIDA's allocation from the government from CAD$3 billion to $1.9 billion. Since the adoption of aid effectiveness policies in the early 2000s, however, CIDA has seen successive increases in its budget of 8% per year, up to a total of more than $3 billion in 2004–2005. By 2010–2011, CIDA had doubled its budget again relative to 2001–2002 levels (CIDA 2009; Sallot 2005).

Calls for trade, not aid, have become the watchwords of many developing countries (notably Uganda and Eritrea) as well as of INGOs, such as Oxfam. Rich countries spent $280 billion in 2004 subsidizing farmers and agribusiness, more than triple the $79 billion they spent on aid (Dugger 2005). The great irony in the debate between aid and trade is that if all trade barriers were removed and agricultural subsidies eliminated, developing countries would gain $100 billion in annual income, according to World Bank estimates, far more than they get in development aid each year. While subsidies and protectionist measures in the European Union and the United States remain a major obstacle for developing economies trying to access these markets, trade in neoliberal development circles points to export-oriented industrialization as an economic strategy, whereby multinational corporations generate foreign currency for the developing country hosting them. The neoliberalization of aid, then, is an extension of the longstanding terms of loans to developing countries through structural adjustment policies.

By neoliberalism I borrow the synthetic meaning of Matthew Sparke's formulation: "a more conjunctural approach to theorizing neoliberalism as a contextually contingent *articulation* of free market governmental practices *with* varied and often quite illiberal forms of social and political rule" (2006, 153; italics in original). Sparke understands neoliberalism ideologically as a regime of governance organized around the themes of (a) liberalizing the capitalist market from state control, and (b) refashioning state practices in the idealized image of the free market, but his analysis also underscores how deregulation in one register can lead to re-regulation in another (see also Amoore 2006). The economic deregulation principles required of developing countries by those bodies that lend them money have long been accompanied by conditions set by the lender. Furthermore, the securitization of aid to prevent unwanted migration is fully commensurate with neoliberal aims of pro-poor growth, except where neoliberal measures displace people from their jobs and homes.

Aid effectiveness is predicated on selectivity, as opposed to the past policy of conditionality whereby a particular set of terms centered around a neoliberal economic policy agenda of fiscal austerity and open markets was attached to aid packages (Pronk 2001). Selectivity instead operates on the basis of actively choosing countries that have a demonstrated commitment to good governance and sound economic policies. Aid is not based on greatest need but on greatest perceived impact or return on funds invested. The reallocation of aid to good performers, advocates say, will produce better results with respect to macroeconomic growth, poverty reduction, and other indicators of development. Boyce (2002) argues, however, that this shift will occur at the expense of "weakly governed" states, the so-called bad performers. "The costs of an indefinite wait-and-see attitude [toward weak states in conflict]—to innocent people within these societies, and to others if the violence spills beyond national borders—may be very high" (Boyce 2002, 242).

Aid effectiveness policy emphasizes government-to-government partnerships and tries to avoid the hierarchal language of donor–recipient. The language of "recipient" has been changed to "host" or "partner government," with ownership by the host country as an apparently new feature of this particular aid approach (CIDA 2001). But Rehman Sobhan argues that the aid effectiveness agenda is actually driven by donors, not host/recipient governments:

Donors remained preoccupied with the effectiveness of development assistance in reducing global poverty. The use of the metric of poverty was inspired by the nature of the appeal to those who finance aid—

> the citizens, largely in the role of taxpayers, in the advanced industrial
> countries (AIC). . . . DC [developing country] aid recipients do not
> vote in AIC elections. (Sobhan 2002, 341–42)

Host governments obviously do not get to select whether they meet the
aid effectiveness criteria. The geographical slippage in accountability and
semantics is important.

Despite all the talk of "empowerment," "partnership," and "participation," development is still something that is defined and enunciated by
the First World. Just as in colonial times, the frameworks and strategies of
development are authored outside of the country concerned, grounded in
foreign (especially neoliberal) ideologies and backed up by the long arm of
debt conditionality (Mercer, Mohan, and Power 2004, 423).

Selecting recipient governments that already have sound economic
policies and stable governments that respect human rights and have low
levels of corruption ensures, in theory, the effectiveness of aid. Aid is, in
a sense, given on the basis of demonstrably shared neoliberal values. This
raises two questions: (1) is the focus of aid on the poorest people in countries most in need of assistance, or on donor imperatives to demonstrate
positive economic growth as a measurable outcome? and (2) is there any
space for poor performers, or even rogue states, to qualify for aid? (*Economist* 2005a). And if not, what might the implications be in relation to
migration, health, and security? While anti-corruption measures and
economic growth are hard to argue against, poverty alleviation is as much
an issue of wealth distribution and access to basic services as of economic
growth. However, foreign aid has never been about addressing poverty
alone. Policymakers, including government officials, must make it appear
politically accountable so that they can increase their access to funds at
home in donor countries.

Santosh Mehrotra (2002) questions the World Bank (1998) report
promoting aid effectiveness, arguing that it "became an ex-post rationali-
zation of what was already a fact—a dramatic reduction in ODA in the
1990s." My take is that aid effectiveness suffers from tautological rea-
soning, explaining past patterns within a framework that fits conve-
niently with the present. Working for the World Bank, Craig Burnside
and David Dollar (2000; 2004) promote the Bank's policy by producing a spate of regression analyses that show a positive relation between

effective institutions and economic "anti-poor" growth. They observe that between 1970 and 1993 countries with good economic policies but low aid payments experienced average growth of 2.2% per capita whereas countries with good economic policies and high aid transfers experienced 3.7% growth, evidence that good policies make a difference, yet how or why this happens is not explained (Cassidy 2002). Other economists have published data that do not fit Burnside and Dollar's model for "pro-poor growth" (Easterly, Levine and Roodman 2003). One of these critics argued, "When you're talking about development, you're talking about wholesale transformation of a society. . . . You're trying to re-create the history of the Western world over the last 200 years, to put other countries through that process. No one knows how to do that" (Roodman quoted in Eviatar 2003).

Nevertheless, the aid effectiveness agenda has taken on an overwhelming momentum. High-level commitments to aid effectiveness have been forged by governments and organizations on all sides of the aid equation (see Table 5.1). Aid effectiveness has become an expression of donor coordination and common strategy.

The Paris Declaration moved the aid effectiveness agenda beyond a set of neoliberal principles to a concrete plan for measuring development

Table 5.1 Aid Effectiveness: High-Level Commitments

Monterrey Consensus (March 2002): Called on developed countries to provide more and better aid, as well as improved trade and debt policies.

Rome Declaration (February 2003): Donors committed to aligning development assistance with partner (recipient) government strategies, and to greater cooperation and harmonization among donors.

Marrakech (February 2004): Heads of the multilateral development banks and chair of the Development Assistance Committee of the OECD affirm commitment to foster global partnerships that "manage for results."

Paris Declaration (March 2005): Ministers of developed and developing countries responsible for development and heads of multilateral and bilateral development organizations signed an international agreement that reaffirmed the commitments of the Rome Declaration and resolved to take far-reaching actions to reform the delivery of aid that could be monitored and managed.

Accra Agenda for Action (AAA) (September 2008): With more input from developing countries, ministers, multilaterals, UN agencies, and civil society representatives met to address three areas where reform is too slow: country ownership, building partnerships, and development results.

Source: Adapted from Graves and Wheeler, 2006: 4; Accra Agenda for Action, 2008

outcomes in 2010, including twelve specific indicators and accountability mechanisms to ensure compliance (OECD 2005; OECD-DAC 2008).[5]

Before turning to the more concrete details of neoliberal aid in Sri Lanka, I briefly reiterate some of the ways in which "security" is construed by donors in a specifically Sri Lankan context. As noted in Chapter 3, development aid has always been an instrument of foreign policy and geopolitical agendas employed to cultivate alliances, provide incentives to purchase donor exports, and promote various facets of state security and economic policies. Aid is no less politicized today than it was during the Cold War when ideological alignment was a tacit aim of development dollars. In the ideological vacuum created at the end of the Cold War, however, new enemies have emerged.

North-South Divides: Geopolitics of Fear and Security

> Widespread poverty and chaos lead to a collapse of existing political and social structures, which would inevitably invite the advance of totalitarianism into every weak and unstable area. . . . Thus our own security would be endangered and our prosperity imperiled. A program of assistance to the underdeveloped nations must continue because the Nation's interest and the cause of political freedom require it. (President John F. Kennedy, 1961 [cited in Cassidy 2002, 66])

While immigration regulations and border controls are the more common sites of securitization, foreign policy and development aid have also become fertile ground for cultivating fear about the proliferation of conflict and its consequences in countries of the global South. As Chapter 3 illustrated, the securitization of fear is part and parcel of state efforts to obtain consent for extraordinary or illiberal measures to minimize security threats. Concerns about international security and state sovereignty are intimately linked to the production of fear at more domestic scales.

The United States, Britain, Canada, the Netherlands, and others have integrated development aid with foreign policy through this parochial security discourse, coupling it with the proviso that aid be given where it can be most effective. Ultimately, governments in these donor countries argue that international cooperation combined with aid effectiveness can make their states more secure. Public anxiety sets in motion political demands for protection from often ill-defined, geographically diffuse threats. Development assistance has, then, become a de facto political tool for engaging countries that are not strategic to donors in terms of foreign policy or trade (Knockaert 2004).[6]

Managing risk through the collection and management of information contained in elaborate databases in the global North is about managing fear of geopolitical threats through a biopolitical approach (Bigo 2002; Amoore 2006; Pain 2009). Fear and insecurity are linked across scales, from the bodies of migrants (Mountz 2010) who represent insecurity in the imagination of states, to the transnational networks of surveillance sited in or on the body (Sparke 2006). Such biopolitical practices include collecting data rooted in retinal scans, fingerprints, and even DNA.

Aid discourse in Canada, Britain, and beyond aims to address poverty in an effort to curb the security risks and costly migration effects of underdevelopment (Duffield 2008). Mobilizing fears of the global South leaking into the global North has become a compelling way to frame development assistance, but it is not the only expression of geopolitics that shapes aid practices today. Other strategic considerations include the role of diaspora in exerting political influence over government aid distributions and the idea that nature has agency and acts in its own right. Development aid has become strategic in new ways.

Neoliberalism Trickles Down to the War Zone: Three Moments

During the Cold War, Sri Lanka maintained a strong position as a non-aligned nation in the Third World, following import substitution policies and eschewing many offers of development aid from the capitalist First World states. This changed dramatically in 1977, when bankruptcy threatened the socialist government of J.R. Jayewardene, who then opened Sri Lanka's markets to export-oriented industrialization and thus had to meet the loan conditions of the IMF. Economic liberalization meant an end to many of the concessions and patronage relations that had kept the peace between otherwise disparate class and ethnic factions;

the glue holding ethnic and class alliances together was effectively removed (Stokke 1998). While foreign dollars began to pour into Sri
Lanka, some Tamil and Sinhala areas remained largely excluded from
investment (Sivanandan 1990, 241). This cultivated intense resentment
among members of the Tamil minority in Sri Lanka's North and Northeast and among rural working-class Sinhala youth in the South.

This new and disparate economic geography was, at least in part,
caused by international aid and loan inputs.

> Here indeed was a deal waiting to be made. But it was implicitly a
> package deal, and one which had visibly to be in place rather quickly.
> Continued support from the World Bank and IMF would implicitly
> be contingent on enthusiasm for Sri Lanka in international business
> circles and in the foreign and trade ministries of the industrialised coun-
> tries. But foreign capital would look at Sri Lanka again only if the new
> government could reverse the country's reputation for political radi-
> calism and electoral instability. Hence a whole series of urgent policy
> measures to create a new business image. (Moore 1990, 354–55)

Mick Moore refutes any causal link between economic liberalization and
violence, but contends that the large net increase of foreign aid that accompanied open markets, along with a larger and more salient public
sector in Sri Lanka, encouraged and sustained authoritarian practices.

Neoliberal economic policies imposed by the IMF nonetheless contributed to the rise of militant nationalism and insurgency by the LTTE
and the JVP. The IMF-promoted neoliberal policies catalyzed exclusion
and arguably conflict in Sri Lanka. The result has been a growing Sri
Lankan Tamil diaspora in Canada, Australia, and many European countries in particular. Three salient moments in the post-1977 context of
neoliberal policies are highlighted below.

The First Moment: From Battleground to Brutalized Bodies

After the 1983 pogroms against Colombo-based Tamils that commonly
mark the beginning of armed conflict in Sri Lanka, intense fighting on
the battlefield between the LTTE and the Sri Lankan armed forces was
exacerbated by acute human rights violations against civilians on the
part of both the Sri Lankan government and the Liberation Tigers of

Tamil Eelam (University Teachers for Human Rights (Jaffna) [UTHR(J)] 1989; Hoole et al. 1990). Canadian government officials, among others, visited Sri Lanka and met with the foreign minister of the day to lobby for the cessation of widespread and well-documented abuses, mostly against Tamil civilians (personal communication 2004). The Sri Lankan government did not respond to Canadian, or any other, pleas and continued its unchecked violence against civilians, actions that cemented Canada's decision to channel all its bilateral aid through NGOs, and not to the government itself (Sri Lanka interview #2, 2002). This arrangement was based on the perceived political neutrality of civil society and an assumption that development funds were more secure in the hands of NGOs.

Many of Sri Lanka's NGOs have a long and reputable history as part of the country's civil society. Two examples, among many, illustrate efforts to address human rights issues through legal and policy approaches. The Law and Society Trust focuses on a variety of issues, from monitoring civil and political rights in the country to documenting wrongful injury and death among humanitarian workers. Another organization, the International Centre for Ethnic Studies (ICES), was once led by specialists in human rights law: Drs. Neelan Thiruchelvam and Radhika Coomaraswamy. Dr. Thiruchelvam was killed by an LTTE suicide bomber while driving to work in 1999. He was Tamil by ethnicity but federalist in principle and by political affiliation. Since 2006 Ms. Coomaraswamy has worked for the United Nations as the special representative for children and armed conflict, having already served as the UN special rapporteur on violence against women. Far more could be said about the important role NGOs, such as the Law and Society Trust or ICES, have played, but the main point is that the NGO sector is well-organized and well-respected by international donors on human rights issues. Canada, in fact, sees this sector as more trustworthy than government when it comes to aid.[7]

Until 2002 CIDA was the only bilateral (or government-to-government) agency operating in Sri Lanka that directed its contribution solely through nongovernmental channels.[8] The line between development aid and humanitarian aid is a geographical one in Sri Lanka, with development programming characterizing the more stable South and humanitarian funding funneled largely to the North and the Northeast for those displaced by the war. Yet the more pressing issues relate to how aid is distributed: during the war it had to go to both government-controlled and LTTE-controlled areas. Acts of aid must also avoid unintentionally fueling the war. One CIDA manager noted, "There is a real risk" that if aid is not equitably distributed among regions and all ethnic groups affected, the conflict in Sri Lanka could be stoked (Canada interview #35, 2005).

Assurances that international assistance will be delivered in a "conflict sensitive" manner are key in this context (Culbert 2005). Bilateral aid to the government of Sri Lanka could always be used to subsidize existing health, education, or social services and funds redirected for defense purposes. Likewise, the LTTE informally "taxed" all goods and services within its territory, including wages and materials for humanitarian and development work, until such practice was defeated in 2009 (see Bastian 2007b; Stokke 2006, 1034). Projects with large capital budgets were at risk of being taxed to an even greater degree.

CIDA recognizes that funding development in a war zone is a difficult undertaking at best, given the risk that funds may be diverted to fuel the conflict either directly or indirectly. "Development success can be a peace-building failure" (Sri Lanka interview #2, 2002). In line with this thinking, CIDA largely avoided funding capital-intensive projects, the conventional bricks-and-mortar approach, opting for knowledge-based training and projects to strengthen institutional and community operations and capacity for more than a decade (CIDA 2003). The WUSC welding project featured in Chapter 4 is one example of an aid program that spends most of its budget on classrooms and hiring teachers, allocating very modest amounts of pocket money to participants to offset transportation and meal costs. Such projects are conflict sensitive: they have smaller budgets with budget line items that are more difficult to divert in the context of war.

Canadian aid to Sri Lanka's civil society organizations has also been bolstered by lobbying on the part of the sizeable Sri Lankan Tamil population in Canada.[9] At more than 250,000 people, Canada hosts the single largest Sri Lankan Tamil diaspora in the world (McDowell 1996). Thus, decisions about aid disbursements can be affected by domestic political considerations in Canada; although by no means internally unified, Canada's "asylum diaspora" (McDowell 1996) wields considerable political influence and does not hold the Sri Lankan government in high regard (Cheran 2000).

This diaspora rapidly emerged in Canada during the late 1980s because of important policy gaps in Canadian refugee processing that contributed to the flow of asylum seekers. In the Singh decision, Canadian courts ruled in 1985 that non-Canadians on Canadian territory have the right to a live refugee adjudication hearing in Canada.[10] The Federal Court of Appeal then ruled Canada's existing refugee process unconstitutional. Amnesty was offered to the 30,000 asylum seekers whose applications were already in the system (personal communication 2004). Without a new system in place, however, a backlog of refugee claimants grew rapidly, rising to 125,000 in 1989. Many applicants were Sri Lankan Tamils who knew about the amnesty. That same year the Immigration and Refugee Board (IRB), a tribunal for hearing refugee claims, was established with a capacity to hear 10,000 claims per year. Acceptance rates among cases in the backlog were high, given the well-documented human rights violations in Sri Lanka at the time. In 2006 the acceptance rate was over 70% for eligible asylum claims made by Sri Lankan Tamils.

Having established the advent of neoliberal policies in Sri Lanka in the late 1970s and the brutal human rights violations and related asylum flows beyond Sri Lanka's borders in the late 1980s and into the 1990s, I want to shift now to the early 2000s when a consensus between international donors and the government of the day emerged. The economic nadir of July 2001 and the CFA of February 2002 created grounds for short-lived peace and prosperity.

The Second Moment: Constructive Engagement

This moment straddles the 2001 airport violence resulting in a plunge into negative economic growth and the 2004 defeat of the pro-peace, pro-neoliberal government of the United National Front (UNF). Some of the salient events that characterize this period have been mentioned: the ceasefire agreement and the advent of internationally mediated peace negotiations between the government and the LTTE, the withdrawal of the LTTE from the negotiations in 2003, and the nonetheless successful international donor conference in Tokyo held later that same year.

Eventually, this window for negotiations closed, despite exceptionally high levels of public support (80%) for government–LTTE talks (Bastian 2007b). This widespread support for change would itself change dramatically with the formation of a new government in 2004.

Until 2001 the Sri Lankan government condemnation of the LTTE as terrorists prevailed due to ongoing violence in the form of suicide bombings. While the government committed its share of violence, this context precluded the possibility of negotiations (Kleinfeld 2007). A lull in the violence and behind-the-scenes overtures of a ceasefire in 2001 led to a political shift in language: from "terrorists" to "non-state actors." The LTTE grew to enjoy much greater legitimacy in this context of negotiations. Once the LTTE relinquished its call for a separate state, and instead asked for greater autonomy within a shared governance structure, the possibility of talks became a concrete option (Kleinfeld 2007).

Increased donor interest in peace and greater stability emerged as grounds for more aid. In this climate, promoting economic incentives for peace became possible. In June 2003, with the prospect of peace in the minds of international donors, the Tokyo conference was held to finance the reconstruction of war-torn Sri Lanka. US$4.5 billion was pledged for the "Regaining Sri Lanka" strategy (Stokke 2006). Most of the big money pledged for reconstruction and rehabilitation came from the IFIs. Bilateral donors continued to focus on peace-building projects and conflict reduction, especially in the North and Northeast (Sri Lanka interview #25, 2005). While the LTTE did not attend, donors nonetheless pledged funds in an effort to create peace dividends. Peace was not a prerequisite to aid; rather, the possibility of peace provided an incentive for it.

However, the UNF government of the day still had to abide by its earlier promises to IFI lenders. The 2004 budget outlined a plan for a long-delayed 30% rollback in public-sector employment over three years. Cuts for the first year would amount to 10%, and these were not popular (Bastian 2007b). The UNF government fell in 2004, replaced by a precarious coalition government that included two Sinhalese nationalist parties, the JVP and the Buddhist monk–led National Heritage Party (*Jathika Hela Urumaya,* JHU). Partnership with these two hardline parties, which saw the Tigers as illegitimate political actors, made it impossible for the government to support renewed negotiations. As well, ceasefire violations escalated in 2004 (J. Perera 2005). These coincided with an internal coup within the LTTE that same year.[11] As prospects for a political settlement diminished, the IFIs returned to supporting the Sri Lankan government, a move that was coupled with further international bans across Europe and in Canada on the LTTE as a terrorist organization (Bastian 2007b).

In Colombo during July 2002 I interviewed the Canadian high commissioner for Sri Lanka, who described Canada's aid role as one of "constructive engagement" whereby Canadian aid had reduced tensions in relation to the conflict and would continue to do so (Sri Lanka interview #18, 2002). Canadian aid, channelled through national NGOs and INGOs like *Médecins Sans Frontières*, would continue to be used for peace-building purposes in a geopolitically non-strategic location. However, after years of working through civil society organizations, Canada added to its aid portfolio and began actively engaging various government ministries in Sri Lanka early in this period, offering considerable in-kind assistance. More directly, CIDA funded experts from the Forum of Federations, a global network on federalism based in Ottawa, to discuss constitutional options, comparative case studies, and prospects for a potentially federalist state (Sri Lanka interview #18, 2002; Chattopadhyay 2002).[12] This aid, coupled with assistance drafting an official languages act, marked a shift from no bilateral aid to high-level in-kind bilateral assistance, but still no hard cash for Sri Lanka government programming (Sri Lanka interview #25, 2005). Very quietly CIDA was trying to wrap up its bilateral programs in Sri Lanka and gradually exit the country altogether.

The Third Moment: Tsunami "Agency" and the Politics of Humanitarian Aid

The tsunami of December 26, 2004, brought about extraordinary destruction for peoples of the Indian Ocean Basin region. In Sri Lanka, more than 36,000 people died, and another 800,000 were displaced from their homes. Many observers point to disparate social relations of exclusion and marginalization that preceded the tsunami and which the tsunami only served to deepen.[13] The enormity of the disaster also begs the question of whether acts of nature shape these social relations and the aid disbursements that followed.

The idea that nature has agency, the power to shape human and non-human relations, has gained considerable currency in the past few years. Geographers in particular have begun to conceptualize nature as part of an "earthlife nexus" (Whatmore 2006, 601) that probes the connections between the *geo* (earth) and the *bio* (life). One way, then, of interpreting the unusually generous aid or to understand post-tsunami social stratification is to explore Whatmore's (2002; 2006) idea of hybrid geographies. Hybrid geographies refer to the relationships between the social and the natural, and the modality of livingness that links them. Whatmore seeks to decouple the subject–object dichotomy through a move from post-structuralist discourse to hybrid practice. Rather than focusing on text and the hearsay of humans, Whatmore focuses on recuperating materiality through close empirical work. I cannot extend the concept of hybrid geographies much further here, except to signal its importance in conducting research on and after the tsunami.

Commenting on Whatmore's 2002 book, Bruce Braun (2005, 835) notes that it is "insistently empirical" to the extent that hybrid geographies shed little light beyond that which is explicitly recounted. This may be a potential shortcoming, but the book's empirical focus is also a strength in the context of ideologically driven debates about aid effectiveness, securitization, and disaster. As Neil Smith (2006) contends, there is no such thing as a natural disaster; the antecedents to (and effects of) every disaster have a human component. Clearly, the agency of natural forces and their intersection with human relations at multiple scales in and beyond disaster zones demand further study.

A Canadian Angle:
Aid Effectiveness Meets Its Match

At the time the tsunami hit, Canada was slowly phasing out smaller bilaterally funded programming in Sri Lanka. During interviews with senior managers at CIDA headquarters in Canada during 2002, I was told that Sri Lanka would be cut from the Canadian aid map when CIDA reduced the number of countries that receive its aid. In accordance with CIDA's aid effectiveness policy, Sri Lanka was considered sufficiently developed to be "graduated" from Canadian aid (Canada interviews #12, #13, June 2002). A transition plan for Sri Lanka was under way to allow CIDA to exit gradually from its bilateral commitments there.

Three years later, the tides had turned: "The tsunami changes everything," said the new Canadian high commissioner for Sri Lanka in a

2005 interview. Canada's exit plan underwritten by aid effectiveness policy was cancelled. She noted that the post-tsunami visit of Prime Minister Paul Martin in January 2005 cemented Canada's and CIDA's role in the country's development for the next decade (Sri Lanka interview #25, 2005).[14] A CIDA vice president in Ottawa (Canada interview #35, 2005) echoed this point and noted that the tsunami was a factor in deciding to include Sri Lanka on CIDA's "top-25" list of development partners in 2005 "because of the global lens" and visibility of the crisis to Canadians. An environmental disaster with the tsunami's scope created remarkable political valence in the context of Canadian aid.

The vice president added that "one of the factors they looked at was diaspora." Sri Lanka made the cut, in part, due to the political influence of the Tamil diaspora in Canada. Nepal, another contender for the spot Sri Lanka received on CIDA's top-25 list, was not selected because "there is no Nepali diaspora in Canada to speak of" (Canada interview #35, 2005). Aid effectiveness and the programming it promotes are not inexorable in the context of developing countries. Forces of nature and distant diasporas can make a difference. In 2009 Canada revisited its core development partners again. This time Sri Lanka failed to make the cut, and aid effectiveness policy prevailed.

Conclusion

Aid effectiveness policy and the quest for pro-poor economic growth are conditioned by political transnationalism, relations with nature, and aspirations for peace. Such neoliberal aid is also shaped by the security agendas of donor states and the perceived insecurity of poorer states. As Gordon Brown, then Britain's chancellor of the exchequer and later its prime minister, said after 9/11, "What happens to the poorest citizen in the poorest country can directly affect the richest citizen in the richest country" (Cassidy 2002, 60). About the same time, [now Sir] Mark Malloch Brown, former head of the UN Development Agency, said, "This [increased aid allocation] is part of the new global arrangement post September 11th. If security is to be maintained, then development policy is going to be just as important as counter-terrorism" (Cassidy 2002, 66). Development aid has long ceased to be a Cold War project of aligning countries of the global South with rival superpowers, nor is it simply a tool of neoliberal capitalist development. Practices of aid are conditioned by debt and war, by diasporas located within governments' political constituencies, and by forces of nature that are sometimes framed as separate from the politics of aid.

The fighting and flagrant human rights violations in Sri Lanka combined with administrative gaps and amnesty by the Canadian government during the late 1980s contributed to the growth of a sizeable Sri Lankan Tamil diaspora in Canada. Now members of this diaspora shape political priorities at CIDA and beyond, and have influenced Sri Lanka's place on the map of Canadian aid. This diasporic twist geographically reworks Walters' (2004) notion of domopolitics, a defensive politics of home, demonstrating that the borders of home are transnational in their reach. In stretching beyond territorial borders, Jeffrey Simpson (2006) observes the immense pressure governments face from immigrant constituencies to take positions on foreign policy and in this case international aid.

Aid is also conditioned by the dynamic demands for capitalist growth, embedded in neoliberal policies and practices on the one hand, and for a rights-based peace on the other. Aid effectiveness policy and the quest for pro-poor economic growth are produced by relations of nature, political transnationalism, and aspirations for peace. When space for talks to end the war emerged, donors embraced the opportunity and pledged unprecedented funds to finance peace with the hope of economic prosperity. In large part, they accepted the LTTE as a legitimate interlocutor during the negotiations, as did the Sri Lankan government, international mediators, and Sri Lankan society. When the talks fell apart, donors shifted back to more conventional aid transfers, supporting the state in its economic expansion.

While the 2004 tsunami in Aceh, Indonesia, catalyzed peace in another case of hybrid geography, the tsunami and the inundation of humanitarian aid that followed created more acrimony than agreement in Sri Lanka. The acts of aid presented here are little more than a historical caricature of the immense archive of (post-)colonial, nationalist, capitalist politics in Sri Lanka, but they demonstrate that aid is a dynamic bundle of geographical relationships at the intersection of war, neoliberalism, nature, and fear.

Notes

1. For a succinct overview of the various phases of the war, see Stokke 2006, 1022.

2. Many Sri Lankan commentators refuse to use "peace" in relation to the ceasefire, preferring instead "not war/not peace" (Bastian 2007b).

3. This sum includes debt-servicing payments and debt forgiveness.

4. The primary research cited draws upon interviews conducted with senior managers of the CIDA at its headquarters in Canada and Sri Lanka, as well as with diplomats and staff at NGOs in both locations in 2002 and 2005. Hence, there is a focus on Canadian aid to Sri Lanka to a greater extent than other donors.

5. The Paris Declaration has been endorsed by more than one hundred countries, twenty-six international organizations, and fourteen civil society organizations (Graves and Wheeler 2006); to read about the indicators and targets for 2010 set out by the Declaration, see OECD 2005 and OECD-DAC 2008.

6. By way of example, "The huge diversion of aid monies into Afghanistan and Iraq is clearly about 'stabilizing' areas that are seen to pose a threat to the North" (Smillie 2004, 15). Canada has sent more development aid to Afghanistan and Iraq than to all of its other aid recipients put together, pledging $600 million between 2001 and 2007 for Afghanistan alone, a significant sum for a donor with an annual budget of just over $3 billion (Knockaert 2004).

7. For more information on the Law and Society Trust, see http://www.lawandsocietytrust.org/, or for ICES, see http://www.icescolombo.org/. Both have operated in Colombo for more than twenty-five years.

8. CIDA's bilateral contribution to Sri Lanka is modest, at roughly CAD$5.5 million per year. This bilateral commitment is not nearly significant enough to put Canada on Sri Lanka's "top-10" list of donors of net official development assistance, topped by Japan (US$167 million) and followed by the Asian Development Bank (US$94 million) and World Bank (US$59 million) (Sriskandarajah 2002). Additional multilateral funds to the ICRC, the Canadian Red Cross, and *Médecins Sans Frontières* (MSF Holland) push total Canadian contributions in Sri Lanka to over CAD$10 million (Sri Lanka interview #17, 2002).

9. As Jeffrey Simpson (2006) notes, wider multiculturalism in Canada brings intensified domestic pressure to take positions on foreign issues and disputes. The Canadian government is more fiercely lobbied than ever by diasporas that want issues in their countries of origin addressed.

10. On April 4, 1985, the Supreme Court of Canada ruled that the Canadian Charter of Rights and Freedoms protects the right of refugee claimants in Canada to life, liberty, and security of the person, and that claimants are thus

entitled to an oral hearing, in accordance with the principles of fundamental justice and international law. This ruling has become known as the "Singh decision" in recognition of Harnhajan Singh, Sadhu Singh Thandi, Paramjit Singh Mann, Kewal Singh, Charanjit Singh Gill, and Indrani and Satnam Singh, who brought their cases to the Court. See Canadian Council for Refugees (2010), accessed June 16, 2010, at http://www.ccrweb.ca/RRDay.htm.

11. In the spring of 2004 the LTTE experienced an unprecedented coup by Tamil Tiger cadres from the East under the breakaway leadership of Karuna. Troops in the North loyal to the LTTE leader Prabakharan were killed by the Karuna faction, which has been accused of assisting the Sri Lankan government's agenda since the split. These political changes have stifled any real progress on the fronts of political reconciliation and peace building.

12. Constitutional expert Dr. Peter Meekison and former Ontario premier Bob Rae (now a Canadian MP) participated in several consultations, although they were held exclusively with the Sri Lankan government.

13. The tsunami of aid that followed the disaster can also be explained as a racialized moment of "it could have been me" (see Olds, Sidaway, and Sparke 2005).

14. Canadian bilateral aid will continue to be disbursed in the unusual manner that has characterized the last fifteen years, whereby no Canadian aid is provided directly to the Sri Lankan government (nor the LTTE) for their use. Rather, all bilateral funds are distributed through NGOs and civil society networks with proven track records.

6

Two Solitudes:
Post-Tsunami and Post-Conflict Aceh

with Arno Waizenegger

Most of the book so far has focused on Sri Lanka. The articulation of peace and disaster in Aceh, Indonesia, also warrants careful interrogation. In August 2005, after the devastating and destructive tsunami in the Indian Ocean Basin, an MoU for the cessation of hostilities between longstanding adversaries, the government of Indonesia and the Free Aceh Movement (GAM), was signed. While peace in Aceh persists, post-conflict relations are still marked by tensions. On a global scale 40% of all civil wars result in post-conflict relapses, and most of these occur within five years after the cessation of armed hostilities (Collier et al., 2006).

For the moment, the coast is clear in Aceh and peace holds more than five years on. While the tsunami did not cause peace in Aceh, it was a major catalyst in what has been called "disaster diplomacy" (Kelman and Gaillard, 2007). International political pressures were an important ingredient in creating conditions for peace, but my collaborator, Arno Waizenegger (see Figure 6.1), and I contend that conditions within Aceh also shaped the peace process.

Probing the link between conflict and disaster, this chapter further analyzes the disjuncture between landscapes of aid for tsunami survivors, on the one hand, and for conflict survivors, ex-combatants, and others reliant on the former conflict economy, on the other. Based on interviews between 2006 and 2009 with government officials, former GAM representatives and fighters, and NGO staff in Aceh, we find that assistance for tsunami survivors has far exceeded that available for conflict

Figure 6.1
Arno Waizenegger,
Co-Author and
Collaborator on
Aceh Research

survivors and ex-combatants. The formation of these two solitudes—the tsunami-affected and the conflict-affected—compound challenges for sustaining peace in Aceh. Our research points to an enduring lack of livelihoods for former rebel fighters and conflict victims that may threaten a sustainable peace.

The analysis that follows explores the intersection of the conflict in Aceh, Indonesia, and the 2004 Indian Ocean Basin tsunami, as well as the extraordinary media attention and aid it brought to bear on the situation. Arno and I identify specific areas affected by these dual disasters of war and tsunami, exposing the very separate flows of aid to those affected. The two disasters overlapped geographically within Aceh Province, but not at the finer scales of coast and hinterland, yet the arrival of international tsunami assistance was in part predicated on the cessation of hostilities to allow for humanitarian assistance.

Most of the international aid provided has been directed toward helping tsunami victims living along the coast. Far more modest assistance has been provided to those most severely affected by the conflict, most of whom live in areas that were not directly affected by the tsunami, a few kilometers farther inland. Human and financial resources for tsunami reconstruction dwarf those for post-conflict recovery and reintegration. While there have been economic incentives for the elites of the former secessionist Free Aceh Movement to encourage political cooperation, the vast majority of demobilized rebels and their families have received very little assistance.

The reintegration of ex-combatants and other groups emerges as one of the most pressing challenges in post-tsunami, post-MoU Aceh, as argued by a representative of the US Agency for International Development in January 2007:

> The government needs to address the reintegration of more than 3,000 ex-combatants, 6,200 GAM non-combatants, 2,000 amnestied prisoners, 2,000 ex-combatants who surrendered prior to the MoU, and 6,500 militia, as well as deal with the 63,000 conflict victims, the

> 2,000 handicapped, and rebuilding 9,149 destroyed houses. . . . There are, however, financial constraints: while almost USD 8 billion is committed to dealing with the aftermath of the tsunami, only USD 200 million is pledged for reintegration efforts. (Hollenbeck 2007)

In field research conducted each year from 2006 to 2009 we probed the articulation of post-tsunami responses and peace negotiations, and aimed to identify the corresponding aid landscapes related to each. In 2007 and 2008, several respondents indicated that grievances were based on a lack of assistance and emerging economic disparities for many former GAM-members. In their eyes, this constituted a potential threat to a hitherto successful peace process.

To what extent, if any, did the tsunami shape the peace process in Aceh? Like the Sri Lankan research, this stage of inquiry sought to ascertain the effect of the tsunami on a politicized landscape of conflict. In Aceh the tsunami and its massive aid infusion did not end the conflict, but they did hasten the process (Le Billon and Waizenegger 2007; Waizenegger and Hyndman 2010). Identifying how the political space for change was created and understanding how it succeeded in consolidating peace in Aceh remains vital to analyzing other conflict-reduction efforts.

This chapter draws on fieldwork with a range of humanitarian and political actors involved in tsunami reconstruction, post-conflict reintegration, and political representation in the transformed post-MoU political landscape. Interviews were conducted in English or in Bahasa Indonesian (by Arno), depending on the informant's preference. Informants involved in the research included various senior GoI officials at the Rehabilitation and Reconstruction Agency for Aceh and Nias, (BRR) and the Aceh Peace-Reintegration Agency (BRA), leaders of all political parties including the newly formed Aceh-based parties, UN representatives, and experts based at local and international NGOs, including a number of civil-society NGOs working on issues of gender, environment, and relief. The research highlights the different geographies of tsunami-affected versus conflict-affected populations, and of aid systems established to respond to the two disasters.

The next section provides some context regarding the pre-tsunami conflict. It is followed by an analysis of the tsunami in relation to the MoU and peace process: basically, the tsunami was a key catalyst, not a cause, of the MoU. It accelerated and amplified the prevalent social and political dynamics toward peace. Next comes an exploration of the production of the "two solitudes," or distinct "aid scapes," for the tsunami-affected on the one hand and for the conflict-affected on the other. Finally, the findings point to the need for increased attention to addressing the reintegration of ex-combatants and the recovery of livelihoods of all victims of the conflict as a constructive measure toward stabilizing Aceh's society.

Antecedents to Conflict and Peace

Aceh has been recognised by world powers as a sovereign state since the sixteenth century. (GAM Prime Minister [in exile] Malik Mahmood, opening speech to the Helsinki Peace Talks, February 22, 2005)

The Indonesian province of Aceh, on the northern tip of Sumatra, is characterized by a long history of resistance to European colonialists and their local allies (Reid 2006). The most recent hostilities were marked by widespread repression and human rights abuses by the conflicting parties, namely the Indonesian Military Forces (*Tentara Nasional Indonesia* [TNI]) and the Free Aceh Movement. These hostilities have lasted for more than three decades and are partly rooted in Aceh's earlier role in the region as well as in its relation to the emerging Indonesian state in the 1940s. For example, when Dutch forces recaptured Indonesia in 1946 after Japan's defeat in the Second World War, Aceh remained the only region of the archipelago free from colonization, pointing to a pronounced political autonomy long before international recognition of Indonesia's sovereignty in 1949.

Discontent triggered armed resistance among the Acehnese elites over the establishment of a secular Indonesian state and Aceh's marginal role in it. President Sukarno succeeded in pacifying the Acehnese through military counterinsurgency as well as through the political concession of reaffirming Aceh's separate provincial status and granting it the additional status of a "special region" (Daerah Istimewa) in 1959 (Wandelt 2005). But Sukarno's political nemesis, Suharto, became president in 1966 and stoked Acehnese discontent during his rule. As noted in chapter 2, feelings of exploitation soared among Aceh's population in 1971, when huge oil and liquid natural gas deposits were discovered near Lhokseu-mawe and Lhoksukon in North Aceh. Exploration was followed by the construction of the biggest refinery in the world at the time, financed as a joint venture between the Indonesian state-owned Pertamina and ExxonMobil (Reid 2006; Ross 2003).

The people of Aceh were largely left out of the royalties and pros-perity that followed from this resource extraction, contributing to the emergence of GAM, an independence movement founded by a small group of Acehnese elites. Its armed struggle was rapidly suppressed by the TNI. With growing battle forces during the ensuing decades, the TNI and GAM committed gross human rights abuses against suspected col-laborators with the enemy party (Schulze 2004; HRW 2001). Within what the TNI considered a context of guerrilla warfare, counterinsur-gency strategies were used to counter GAM. Yet this practice fueled hatred and nationalism among a large part of Aceh's population against Indonesian rule and the army. In turn, this anger sustained recruitment and support for GAM's armed resistance (Sukma 2004).

Against this background of secessionist ambition, characterized by nationalism and widespread poverty, the tsunami that hit the coasts of war-torn Aceh cost the lives of about 167,000 people (4% of Aceh's pop-ulation). Almost half a million more were displaced (15% of the popu-lation), and the already miserable humanitarian, social, and economic situation in the province dramatically worsened due to the tsunami (BRR and Partners 2005; GoI 2005; TEC 2006). The then newly elected Indonesian president Susilo Bambang Yudhoyono declared the catastrophe a "national disaster" the following day (GoI 2006) and requested mili-tary restraint. GAM also committed to a unilateral ceasefire to facilitate relief operations. The final MoU document, in fact, states, "The parties are deeply convinced that only the peaceful settlement of the conflict will enable the rebuilding of Aceh after the tsunami disaster on 26 December 2004 to progress and succeed" (Awaludin and Mahmud, 2005). Ensuing official negotiations between GAM and the Indonesian government, which had been secretly prepared before the tsunami, led to a more sta-ble cessation of hostilities after the Memorandum of Understanding for peace was signed on July 15, 2005 (Merikallio 2005; ICG 2005a, 2005b; *Tempo* 2005).

The Historical Context of Acehnese Nationalism

Acehnese nationalism is rooted in its political economy and in struggles and conflict with the Indonesian central government. Hasan di Tiro is a descendant of the last sultan of Aceh and a direct descendant of Teuku Cik di Tiro, a famous Acehnese national hero of the Aceh War (1873–1903). Hasan di Tiro owned Doral International, an oil conglomerate that lost exploration rights for the oil and gas deposits on Aceh's east coast against a joint venture between the state-owned oil company Pertamina, the Indonesian military, and ExxonMobil. His defeat in the oil deal, along with a lack of adequate repatriation of royalties from Aceh's extractive industries, was seen as a renewed expression of the unjust Javanese exploitation and domination of the province (Barter 2004). This perceived slight served to reinforce the native elite's strong ethno-nationalist sentiments. As a former supporter of the Darul Islam Rebellion[1] in 1976, di Tiro initiated the Aceh–Sumatra National Liberation Front (ASNLF), commonly known as the Free Aceh Movement, which issued its Declaration of Independence of Aceh–Sumatra.[2] After numerous skirmishes with the TNI and heavy human rights abuses by both sides, di Tiro and most of his surviving followers fled to Sweden and established an exile government in 1979 (Schulze 2003). This exile government remained in place and was vital in the peace negotiations, culminating in the signing of the MoU for peace in 2005, more than twenty-five years later.

Before the MoU, several political issues festered between GAM and the GoI. Lack of access to oil and gas revenues continued. The transmigration of Javanese settlers to Aceh was seen as a tactic by the central government to "Indonesianize" its rebellious province.[3] The GoI's lack of respect for Aceh's distinct cultural and religious customs generated distrust. The politics of impunity and massive human rights abuses by Indonesian government forces in 1989–1998 (the Military Operations Zone or "DOM" period) increased resentment among the population of Aceh and sustained the secessionist struggle (Sukma 2004; Human Rights Watch [HRW] 2001). While GAM was initially a small and poorly equipped guerrilla group that was rapidly suppressed by the Indonesian military, it increasingly challenged the Indonesian government's control of the province during DOM—and that despite a ratio of roughly one GAM rebel for every fifteen government troops (Ross 2003) (see Table 6.1).

This challenge was rooted in GAM's strategy of internationalization, which included leadership and funding from the political–military diaspora in Sweden, training in and funding from Libya between 1986 and 1989 (Schulze 2003; Ross 2003) and the supply of arms from Cambodia, Thailand, and India (Wandelt 2005; Aceh interview #25, 2006). Starting in 1997 GAM sought the international attention of allies in the conflict while trying to pressure the GoI into peace negotiations. In persisting with internationalization as a political strategy, GAM aimed to gain the best bargaining position possible for its struggle for independence (Aceh interview #37, 2006). After 2000 GAM succeeded with this strategy (Schulze 2004); the TNI's goal, however, was to eliminate the separatist movement (General Suharto cited in Sukma 2004, 24) or to force GAM into accepting the offers of Jakarta (Miller, 2006).

The Financial Crisis and East Timor's Separation From Indonesia

The fall of President Suharto from power in May 1998 ushered in greater openness and hope that the conflict in Aceh could be resolved. His departure was precipitated in part by the financial crisis in Southeast Asia, but also by the end of the Cold War and a new geopolitical distance introduced by allies such as the United States, which had earlier turned a blind

Table 6.1 Key Events, Casualties, and GAM Strength in Aceh

Phase	I: 1976–1979	II: 1989–1991	III: 1999–2005			
Key Events	Founding of GAM	DOM/ Military Operations Zone	Humanitarian Pause, 2000–2001	Cessation of Hostilities Agreement, December 2002– May 2003	Martial Law/ State of Emergency, May 2003– May 2005	MoU, Aug. 2005
Casualties	100	2,000–10,000		5,000		
GAM Strength	25–200	200–750	15,000–27,000			

Source: World Bank staff estimates (World Bank, 2006a)

eye to Indonesia's domestic human rights abuses. Although the financial disaster in much of Southeast Asia did lead to a suspension of hostilities and greater self-rule for Aceh, these effects were only temporary.

In 1999, following a referendum, East Timor gained independence, separating from Indonesia. Then president Abdurrahman Wahid, who took power in Indonesia in October 1999, fueled separatist expectations of the Acehnese by raising the possibility of a referendum on the status of Aceh. GAM members began to return from exile and hideouts in support of the referendum, and GAM seemed to become more and more "like a government in waiting" (Reid 2006, 28). Student organizations coalesced to form the Centre for an Aceh Referendum (*Sentral Informasi Referendum Aceh,* SIRA) and held pro-referendum rallies (McCulloch 2005; Aguswandi 2004a).

With pressure from hard-line Indonesian nationalist military actors and limited political will for such change in Jakarta, however, Wahid withdrew his offer of a referendum on Aceh. Despite peace talks facilitated by the Swiss-based NGO Henry Dunant Centre (HDC)[4] and the signature of a "humanitarian pause" agreement in May 2000 between the GoI and GAM, hostilities resumed within months (Kay 2003). Under President Wahid, the TNI launched a new security operation against GAM after attacks on ExxonMobil in April 2001 that forced the company to shut down its operations (Sukma 2004; Iyer and Mitchell 2004).

President Megawati Sukarnoputri came to power on July 23, 2001, and passed special autonomy legislation No. 18, designed by Wahid, which included Aceh's right to a greater share of natural resource revenue. The legislation also included Aceh's right to implement sharia law and set up sharia courts, to create symbols of autonomous government, and to rename the province Nanggroe Aceh Darussalam (McCulloch 2005). In December 2002 renewed peace talks brokered by the Henry Dunant Centre resulted in the Cessation of Hostilities Agreement (CoHA). This established a Joint Security Committee with representatives from both the TNI and GAM, as well as a team of Southeast Asian monitors. Despite sporadic clashes, peace zones were declared and international aid pledges for reconstruction made in the event that the CoHA succeeded (Prasodjo and Hamid 2005). Final peace negotiations by the Joint Security Committee in May 2003 failed, and President Megawati immediately declared martial law in Aceh. One year later, this edict was replaced by a state of civil emergency.

The TNI then embarked on the largest military operation since East Timor, with 40,000 troops and 12,000 police shipped to Aceh. It again aggravated the conditions of the Acehnese people, killing thousands and, according to the human rights NGO Tapol (2004), displacing at least 125,000 persons.[5] Aceh was closed to independent human rights groups, journalists, and foreign citizens (Laksono 2005). The TNI controlled the public sphere in Aceh. Local media and civil society movements were strongly impeded by a repressive administration (Suud 2005). Nevertheless, segments of civil society continuously lobbied—mainly via the Internet and through exiled activists in foreign countries—for national and international political involvement to find a peaceful solution to the conflict.[6]

During 2004, however, attention to the conflict in Aceh declined due to the presidential elections campaign: "the war in Aceh has become a forgotten war, internationally and in Indonesia" (Tapol 2004). On the ground, GAM's capacity to do battle was strongly impeded when the TNI killed 6,000—or about one-quarter of—GAM combatants plus thousands of people associated with GAM (ICG 2005a; Nessen 2006; Aceh interview #37, 2006). GAM's extensive supply, intelligence, and political networks—which were critical to its guerrilla-style warfare— substantially broke down, and GAM ran short of weapons, ammunition, and equipment (Aceh interview #37, 2006).

As a consequence, GAM was pushed out of the cities and villages and into the forests (Pan 2005). During the second half of 2004 GAM was forced to retreat into a defensive position (Aceh interview #37, 2006). Although this situation never threatened GAM's survival, numerous commanders were keen for an exit strategy from the conflict (Pan 2005). The general mood among Aceh's population and its belief in future peace were dampened by the collapse of CoHA, on the one hand, and by TNI's increasing local presence and power, on the other, but the common aim of most people in Aceh was still to abandon terror and forge peace. Consequently, "A large part of the Acehnese people who formerly supported GAM became neutral in their position towards the conflicting parties. Most of the people were just longing for peace" (Aceh interview #17, 2006). However, political transformation precipitated by the financial crisis of 1998 had created a context of constraints that led to the failure of peace initiatives before the tsunami.[7]

The change of presidential leadership in Indonesia, from Megawati to General Susilo Bambang Yudhoyono, gave Acehnese people a small glimpse of hope and finally proved to be favorable to a new peace process.[8] First elected in September 2004 and having directly dealt with the Aceh conflict as minister of politics and security under President Megawati, Yudhoyono wanted to end the conflict in Aceh (Neuwirth et al. 2006; Askandar 2006). Yudhoyono appeared more sincere about pursuing a negotiated outcome than any of his predecessors. During his campaign, he offered serious political participation and amnesty to GAM in exchange for accepting autonomy rather than independence.

To achieve this compromise, he assigned Vice President Jusuf Kalla, a former minister of Megawati and the leader of the Golkar party, to engage in dialogue with GAM. Furthermore, thanks to Yudhoyono's strong and popular mandate, he won 78% of the vote in Aceh in his first bid for president.[9] With the trust he received from the parliamentary majority, the president was in a unique position to introduce profound political change in Aceh. Finally, Yudhoyono's connection to and influence over the military proved to be an asset rather than a liability, since these links gave the government greater control over the TNI. In the context of Indonesia's continued democratization and decentralization, these conditions created space for political change before the tsunami hit.

When the tsunami hit, a GAM rebel leader and political opponent of the government of Indonesia, Irwandi Yusuf, was in Keudah Prison in Banda Aceh. As his cell was flooded, he was one of 40 prisoners to get safely out of the prison on December 26, 2004. Some 238 others perished in the locked facility as it filled with water (Mydans 2007). In 2006 Irwandi was elected governor of Aceh, and Muhammad Nazar, the former head of a GAM-sympathetic organization, SIRA, became his vice governor.[10] The first provincial elections were held in April 2009. Then, in mid-2007 a new party formed in Aceh (*Partai Aceh* [PA]), mainly made up of former members and supporters of GAM, won these elections in a landslide. Most of the seats in the Aceh provincial parliament are now held by members or sympathizers of the former guerrilla movement.

Since the MoU, the number of reported incidents of criminal violence has gradually and continually risen, while conflicts between GAM and the TNI and police have dropped dramatically. A dramatic surge in criminal violence occurred during the campaign in the run-up to the provincial elections in 2009. However, following PA's victory, violence has substantially decreased (CPCRS 2009b, 2) (see Table 6.1). The newly inaugurated PA legislators are now under heavy pressure to live up to the expectations of their constituencies. President Susilo Bambang Yudhoyono, hailed as Aceh's peacemaker, was reelected in 2009 with strong support from Aceh (more than 93%, the highest among all Indonesian provinces). Hence, the national political situation has further consolidated five years of peace in Aceh (CPCRS 2009b, 2a, 2f).[11]

Tsunamis for Peace:
Disaster Diplomacy and the MoU of 2005

> President Yudhoyono and the leaders of Free Aceh Movement turned the tragedy of the tsunami into an opportunity—an opportunity to build peace in Aceh. (Former UN secretary-general Kofi Annan, 2006 [cited in Mangkusubroto and Sugiarto 2007])

Kelman and Gaillard (2007) describe "disaster diplomacy" as the extent to which disaster-related activities—including prevention and mitigation activities or response and recovery—induce cooperation between enemy parties on national or international scales.[12] In relation to Aceh, these authors use specific criteria to determine whether disaster diplomacy made a difference. Consistent with other analyses of conflict and disaster, Kelman and Gaillard contend that disaster-related activities frequently catalyze diplomatic progress, but rarely create it. The authors note that the tsunami, and the relief and reconstruction operations that followed, opened up Aceh to the world, ending the province's government-imposed isolation and invisibility. In Aceh, the tsunami created new political space for change (Le Billon and Waizenegger, 2007). The seeds of peace, however, were already in place before December 26, 2004, as longstanding secret negotiations between the conflicting parties had already culminated in an agreement to official peace talks four days before the tsunami struck (Merikallio 2005; ICG 2005a; *Tempo* 2005).[13] Kelman and Gaillard argue persuasively that international involvement fostered a call for a ceasefire so that post-tsunami aid could reach Aceh. The international community facilitated the peace talks and supported the

European Union (EU)–Association of Southeast Asian Nations (ASEAN) collaboration to monitor the peace agreement.

This chapter does not dispute that analysis, but posits that the political and economic landscape inside Aceh was also transformed after the tsunami and is important in explaining the political transformation. Social, cultural, and political considerations on the ground conditioned prospects for peace in a number of ways. In the interviews conducted in June 2007, all but one respondent observed a strong connection between the impact of the tsunami and the attainment of an MoU for peace. They regarded the tsunami as a "key to change," a "chance for peace," an "exit plan from the war," as "helping," "contributing," and "supportive to the peace process." The tsunami created suffering that in turn motivated the parties in conflict "to sit together" alongside the population and to bring the war to an end.

In most instances, the tsunami was religiously interpreted as *vonis* (punishment) for Aceh and Indonesia for waging war, with the peace agreement constituting the *hikmah* (lesson and blessing) drawn from this punishment. Without the tsunami, the majority of informants maintained that conflict would have gone on for years.

Interviewees were asked, "What effect did the tsunami have on the peace process?" A pattern emerged in their responses:

> GAM looked at the humanitarian side and decided it could not go on. The Indonesian government saw the same; regardless of if they wanted to or not, they had to sign the MoU. (Ex-GAM commander, now representative of the Aceh Transition Committee [*Komite Peralihan Aceh*, KPA])[14] (Aceh interview #201, 2007)
>
> The seeds were already planted pre-tsunami in 2000. We need to see that the peace agreement follows through for five to ten years, not just two years as we have now. (NGO lawyer) (Aceh interview #202, 2007)
>
> The general direction for peace was there but the tsunami helped a lot. (NGO trainer doing reintegration work) (Aceh interview #205, 2007)
>
> Yes, the tsunami made a difference. . . . GAM leadership in Sweden had a change of heart post-tsunami. (Senior member of the KPA) (Aceh interview #208, 2007)
>
> Thanks to the tsunami, Indonesia is willing to embark on change. . . . The tsunami is the key to change the fences between Jakarta and Aceh. (Leader of a newly formed political party) (Aceh interview #213, 2007)

Many of these responses were moving testimonies to the markers of loss, devastation, and shock created by the tsunami. Asked why peace has held much longer this time than in previous times, many respondents mentioned the tsunami as a factor.

The economic dimensions of the tsunami also contributed to promoting a resolution of the conflict, notably by providing a peace dividend to the elite of GAM in particular (Waizenegger 2007). A peace dividend is simply the allocation of some form of reward as a result of the cessation of hostilities. Besides private business opportunities in the reconstruction business[15] (Aditjondro 2007), rewards included posts for some high-ranking "political" GAM with the national reconstruction and reintegration bodies, BRR and BRA, respectively. The provision of such posts was agreed upon in the 2005 MoU: "GAM will nominate representatives to participate fully at all levels in the commission established to conduct the post-tsunami reconstruction (BRR)" (GoI and GAM 2005, 1.3.9). While "buying peace" through the support of the former rebel elite has helped to bring about some stability at the outset of the peace process, the inequitable manner in which rewards have been allocated has eroded newfound unity and harmony in Aceh's society by creating a divide between haves and have-nots five years on.

The task of reintegrating ex-combatants and implementing measures aimed at post-conflict recovery is the responsibility of the BRA, which was established in February 2006 by Aceh's local administration. Besides compensating former rebels, this agency was also tasked with distributing compensation for victims of the conflict and for rehabilitating public and private property destroyed or damaged as a consequence of the conflict. Having little experience and few skills in the field of its mandate, the BRA has been denounced for its generally poor performance and for lacking policy direction, expert knowledge on reintegration, transparency, and accountability (Beek 2007; ICG 2007). Potential beneficiaries were confused, angry, and dissatisfied with the BRA as procedures kept shifting and proposals were frequently not accepted for any verifiable reason. Many of the allocated funds were not spent efficiently, and some funds fell prey to corruption. By mid-2008 the agency had disbursed funds to 5,726 conflict-affected villages, with disbursements ranging from $6,500 to $18,000 (Rayan 2007).

Problems regarding the reintegration of former combatants were anticipated at the outset of BRA's formation. The authors of the MoU text did not consult with experts on reintegration, and underestimated the number of GAM rebels for political reasons (Avonius 2007).[16] An overburdened BRA and its "protectionist attitude" against foreign advice and cooperation (Aceh interview #322, 2008), as well as a general delay in the delivery of funds by the GoI, made things worse.

In addition to the peace dividends, the geographical and temporal aspects of the tsunami disaster contributed to the resolution of the conflict. Unlike in Sri Lanka, where spaces of high-intensity conflict and severe tsunami impact coincided directly (on Sri Lanka's east coast), Aceh's spaces of disaster were more separate. The dual disasters—the tsunami and the conflict—overlapped in Aceh Province, but the former was a more coastal phenomenon and the latter a more inland concern. This situation was favorable to the peace process because it reduced the risk of direct competition for aid and the politicization of relief by the warring parties (Le Billon and Waizenegger 2007).

As noted, the rapid onset of the tsunami helped bring about a high degree of general attention and scrutiny to Aceh and Indonesia, thus supporting a more urgent resolution of the conflict. Finally, and most important, the timing of the tsunami (shortly after the conflicting parties agreed to official negotiations) was beneficial to catalyzing the ongoing effort to find a political solution.

As Naomi Klein (2007) reminds us, Milton Friedman's crisis hypothesis has so far proven to be right: "Only a crisis—actual or perceived—produces real change. When that crisis occurs, the actions that are taken depend on the ideas that are lying around" (Friedman and Friedman 1982, ix). In this case, "lying around" meant a commitment to peace, a will for peace that was already present before the tsunami but which the tsunami made more urgent. The crisis was then used to leverage political change to stop the conflict. The rehabilitation and reconstruction process has fostered and secured the peace process and led to a dramatic decrease in everyday violence compared to wartime. In particular, the internationalization of the disaster along with the massive influx and presence of foreign eyes and ears in Aceh has galvanized political stability.

Yet more than five years after the tsunami, we argue that the two separate aid scapes persist in Aceh, and have also contributed to increasing levels of crime, violence, and social tensions in the province.[17] These tensions include economic grievances, jealousy, and frustration among those in need who are still struggling with the psychological and economic consequences of armed conflict and its termination, as well as those who find themselves deprived of assistance despite the massive aid intervention. Generous help for the tsunami victims and sweet deals for many former higher-ranking GAM members have created a class of post-crisis winners, but also a clear class of losers who see themselves excluded from the disaster dividend (see Figure 6.2).

Disjointed Disaster Landscapes— Disjointed Aid Landscapes

The destruction the tsunami visited upon Aceh was catastrophic, yet "in many ways conflict-affected areas have experienced more extensive [but less graphic] damage than the tsunami-affected areas" (World Bank

Figure 6.2 Woman in Front of Her Home Rebuilt by Turkish Red Crescent Society in Lampuuk Village, West of Banda Aceh

2007, 88). The conflict has displaced more families from their villages than the tsunami. Despite the money and assistance readily available for tsunami reconstruction, relatively few funds exist to integrate ex-GAM rebels and to rehabilitate infrastructure, houses, livelihoods, and health infrastructure for other survivors of the conflict.

After the tsunami struck the coastlines of Aceh in late 2004, eight months passed before the warring parties agreed to peace. Wary of international involvement during a period of ongoing armed conflict, the GoI and the TNI initially restricted access to conflict areas. Unfortunately, these restrictions on all foreign agencies largely precluded aid delivery to the conflict-affected areas. In locations where conflict and tsunami camps for the displaced neighbor each other, it was "strictly forbidden to let any assistance cross the line between 'humanitarian' tsunami IDPs [internally displaced persons] and 'political' conflict IDPs" (Aceh interview #308, 2008).

Yet after the MoU was signed and some restrictions lifted, few foreign aid agencies were open to the idea of also assisting conflict victims not affected by the tsunami. Cautious in their diplomatic relations with Indonesia, bilateral and multilateral organizations in particular were still very consciously keeping the conflict issue operationally and geographically out of their aid delivery programs. Most of the INGOs that came to Aceh after the tsunami were not even aware of the conflict context: "many actually came and left and never understood that at all" (Aceh interview #330, 2008). Of the agencies that became aware of the needs of conflict victims, few were willing or able to do something about it.

In contrast to bilateral or multilateral aid agencies, INGOs and their local partners could, in theory, act much more independently. Nonetheless, they faced another paralyzing restriction: donor intent. Their funding was earmarked for tsunami-related needs only. Most of the few agencies also assisting "only" conflict-affected persons were NGOs that had experience working in Aceh before the tsunami. They were aware of the fate of the conflict victims and thus made sure funds were not exclusively used to assist tsunami victims.[18]

Whereas the tsunami preceded the cessation of armed conflict and had its most graphic impacts on the north and west coasts of Aceh, the conflict was most intense along Aceh's east coast (BRR and Partners 2008; Good et al. 2006; Humanitarian Information Centre [HIC] and

Office for the Coordination of Humanitarian Affairs [OCHA] 2005). As a result, international tsunami aid did not touch the poverty and destruction inflicted by the conflict over the preceding decades. The good news of peace in the wake of the tsunami, in contrast to the very graphic bad news of the tsunami itself, has largely concealed the devastated livelihoods and hardships inflicted on people by a relatively "ordinary" war.

The peace process gained ground in early 2006, and by the middle of that year most of the large aid agencies had become aware of emerging disparities in the level of needs versus assistance of each disaster-affected population. Nevertheless, by mid-2007 very few agencies had lifted restrictions to extend their project areas beyond the immediate coastline to assist the victims of the conflict.[19]

Polarization of the Disaster-Affected: Tsunami Versus Post-Conflict Survivors

Public concern about the mismatch of aid to tsunami-related needs versus conflict-related needs did not crystallize until more than two years after the tsunami. The head of BRR, Kuntoro Mangkusubroto, then stressed the need to integrate post-tsunami rehabilitation and reconstruction programs with post-conflict reintegration programs. At the Coordination Forum for Aceh and Nias in April 2007 in Jakarta, he asked, "How can we only carry out reconstruction process in coastal areas, while 5 kilometers away there is an area destroyed by conflict?" (*Serambi* 2007). He declared, "In the future, the two must be rebuilt in an integrated way" (*Serambi* 2007). At the same time, however, he acknowledged that so far donors had expressed their commitment and contribution only to post-tsunami rehabilitation and reconstruction programs.

The exclusive and enormous post-tsunami reconstruction and rehabilitation effort has exacerbated longstanding disparities in development patterns between the relatively prosperous coastal areas and the underdeveloped hinterland. Although livelihoods and job opportunities are still the main priority for people affected by the dual disasters (World Bank 2007), those affected by the end of conflict are particularly disadvantaged. Where people are unskilled in activities other than warfare, unemployment and poverty are especially grave.

In 2006, 75% of the ex-combatants in Aceh were still unemployed (World Bank 2006b). Two years later, the situation largely remained unchanged. Among the persons interviewed for this study in June 2007, insufficient economic reintegration of ex-combatants remained a critical issue with regard to peace in Aceh: "The priority is jobs and reintegration funds. The MoU stipulates this, but only 3 to 4% has been allocated," complained a KPA spokesperson (Aceh interview #115, 2007). Most of the 15,000 GAM ex-combatants have not had regular work since the MoU was signed in 2005.

Many former GAM members—including combatants, noncombatants, and prisoners given amnesty—are frustrated (Aceh interview #208, 2007). In the town of Sigli, about a ninety-minute drive east of Banda Aceh, a meeting was held with fourteen working-class men who had fought for GAM or who had gone to Malaysia, either for work as laborers or for political protection. Those living in Malaysia had returned after the tsunami, hoping that they would find work at home. Twelve of the fourteen men said they were less satisfied with and "more sad" about their situation in 2007 than they were during the conflict. Most spoke of plans to start businesses or small farms, but none had the capital to do it, echoing Hollenbeck's (2007) findings.[20]

No Land in Sight for Former Combatants

The gulf between the specific needs and levels of assistance provided to each disaster-affected community has grown as problems in post-conflict Aceh have emerged. Besides a boost in the number of local conflicts along the east coast (the former stronghold of GAM and place of origin of many GAM leaders),[21] reported incidents of petty crime, robberies, kidnappings, and extortion have steadily increased,[22] indicating dissatisfaction and persistent economic pressures (World Bank/DSF 2007a; ICG 2007; Associated Press 2008; *Serambi* 2008a).[23]

Deprived of assistance and job opportunities, many former combatants have resorted to raising funds illegally, a skill they acquired during conflict (Aspinall 2008). Referring to the cumulative incidents of extortion, threats, and rip-offs that most operational aid agencies had to face, a program manager of an international NGO asserts,

> I think this is mainly a result of the uneven and the unjust way aid often was distributed combined with high prices due to inflation. Some did not receive anything, so they just try to take it by other means. (Program manager of a nongovernmental humanitarian agency) (Aceh interview #328, 2008)

Reintegrating former combatants into society by ensuring livelihood recovery and social security is one of the most pressing issues complicating a hitherto stable peace process.

Demobilized soldiers represent a security problem if they do not receive adequate official support in the wake of the conflict or if they lack access to alternative livelihoods, especially if they are returning to impoverished families. In Indonesian culture, this danger has been expressed in the term *preman*, which originally referred to irregular or demobilized soldiers[24] (Ryter 2000). Today, the word is used in reference to (political) "gangsters" or "bandits" often associated with the extortion of illegal rents or involvement in illegal businesses or related conduct (Lindsey 2001). Such extortion is reflected in the current aid landscape in Aceh (*Serambi* 2008b).

An abundance of tsunami aid is easy prey for many former combatants in an environment with low levels of legal enforcement. This climate is reinforced by the pressure on many affluent aid organizations to realize goals in an expeditious manner, and thus that turn a blind eye to corruption, extortion, and bribes in order to secure the smooth implementation of projects. Besides these informal "taxes," fierce and often violent competition for employment, contracts, and sales are symptoms of this highly funded aid environment. Many former fighters participating in this race are increasingly comfortable relying on the "fast money" of the development industry (Aceh interviews #320 and 333, 2008; Aspinall 2008).

In accordance with the MoU, the GoI has provided some funds to compensate former rebels and other victims of the conflict. The GoI allocated about $200 million in total for 2005 to 2007.[25] Yet reintegration and conflict recovery have proven to be more difficult problems than the disarmament and demobilization of former combatants that, monitored by the Aceh Monitoring Mission (AMM), went relatively smoothly. In 2008 reintegration remained one of the major challenges for the local authorities with regard to sustainable peace in the province.[26]

By 2009 most of the international aid money for tsunami reconstruction and rehabilitation had been spent, and the majority of international agencies involved in reconstruction had gone home. Access to the gravy train of abundant aid, through both legitimate and illicit channels, has declined precipitously. How the livelihoods of former rebel fighters evolve, and whether the end of tsunami aid creates new tensions, remains to be seen.

Conclusion

The 2004 tsunami was an exceptional opportunity for political collaboration in Aceh since it created practical grounds for peace, namely the creation of a more stable and safe situation for post-tsunami reconstruction. This, in turn, added to the pre-tsunami political will of both warring parties to find a solution to the conflict. The tsunami catalyzed an already in-progress peace initiative and internationalized the peace-building process by exposing and publicizing the conflict to a concerned audience that was willing to provide the Aceh Monitoring Mission and a massive international presence. For GAM, this ensured a favorable bargaining position as well as greater accountability and commitment to potential agreements with the GoI. The sympathy and solidarity factors as well as the psychological impact of this catastrophic disaster helped bring about the peace agreement between GAM and the GoI and consolidated the best chance of durable peace in Aceh since the foundation of GAM.

Economic and social injustices between the national center (Jakarta and Java) and the provincial periphery (Aceh) fueled three decades of conflict between the GoI and GAM. Since the devastating tsunami of December 2004 catalyzed the cessation of these hostilities, new tensions have emerged, this time within Aceh. These tensions are partly the result of aid allocation in response to the dual disasters of tsunami and conflict. Two largely separate aid scapes emerged for each of the humanitarian crises, with the attention, expertise, and resources allocated for tsunami victims far exceeding those for survivors of the conflict. As a result, more than five years after the tsunami, many conflict victims—including ex-combatants—are still disadvantaged by a lack of health care, access to education and information, and in particular, job skills and opportunities.

In contrast, tsunami survivors and high-ranking members of the former armed groups have profited massively from Aceh's lucrative aid

industry. While much of that aid has stopped flowing, the social grievances relating to disparities in the allocation of attention, funds, and effective assistance have left a legacy of political tensions in Aceh's society.

Many ex-combatants and families affected by the end of conflict are
frustrated and feel neglected in light of both massive assistance toward
the victims of the tsunami and the fact that some of "their own" senior
GAM commanders have emerged, through patronage and acts of "dis-
honest behaviour," with disproportionate benefits (Aceh interview #202,
2007; see also Palmer 2007). In order to reduce social injustices and tensions in Aceh, the government has the difficult task of addressing general
conflict-induced underdevelopment as well as high levels of violence,
crime, and related feelings of insecurity and fear.

International post-tsunami assistance was crucial for catalyzing peace
and fostering its continuation. However, since the MoU, a less exclusive
approach to post-tsunami recovery and rehabilitation could help to avoid
some of the emerging problems by considering the rather similar needs
of conflict victims. This research provides evidence that greater emphasis
on the reintegration of conflict-affected communities through improved
livelihoods is warranted. Furthermore, the integration of analysis and
response to the two disaster aid scapes is critical to avoiding these short-
comings during future dual disasters.

This chapter has argued that responses to and resources for the
tsunami and for the end of the conflict signaled by the MoU were geographically and operationally separate in Aceh, creating disparities and
tensions in their wake. A more coordinated approach that combined
these distinct aid resources and targeted all victims of the dual disasters
could have avoided the stark disparities between tsunami survivors and
those affected by the end of conflict. Nonetheless, peace persists, Kuntoro
Mangkusubroto (2009), the head of BRR, said on New Year's Day 2009:

> The challenge of recovery in such circumstances is anything but easy.
> But, as we have shown over the past four years, it is possible. With the
> enormous financial generosity and technical support of the interna-
> tional community . . . we have built back—and done so to a better
> standard than before the tsunami and earthquake.
>
> The raw figures are impressive: 118,000 new houses, almost
> 3,000km newly-laid roads, over 100,000 hectares of reclaimed agri-
> cultural land, over 900 new health facilities and more—all in less than
> four years.

This is the good news, the official news. The dark side of humanitarian aid is less celebrated, and the bad news rarely recounted. The stories of migrant laborers from Java hired to build these houses by contractors employed by the international aid organizations in Aceh are more sobering (Grandfield 2010). Many were never paid fully or at all for their work. The INGOs simply did not have the capacity to oversee the reconstruction directly, so in many cases they subcontracted. In so doing, they ceded control of projects and encountered some of the same problems that private corporations that contract smaller firms often face: unsavory and sometimes illegal labor practices.

Evidence that the tsunami hastened the signing of a peace agreement is clear. How aid agencies, most of which have either tsunami-related or conflict-based mandates, can address the effects of these dual disasters in an integrated manner and in concert with the government of Aceh remains an open question. Echoing one activist based at a local humanitarian NGO, this research finds that prospects for more justice and for a "less violent peace" in Aceh rely on the answer:

> I assure [you] that if the perspective on the way that aid is delivered changes, I think that peace in Aceh will really be lasting because the people feel that this peace becomes a possession of the people where all get a benefit from this peace, which will then be commonly protected. But, with a continuous perspective on victims which differentiates between conflict victims and tsunami victims, there will always be someone feeling disadvantaged in the current process. And I fear that this causes again jealousy, as it already existed during conflict time. (Aceh interview #340, 2008)

Peace may be holding, but Dahlman's (2009) idea that "post-conflict" refers to war by other means seems prescient here. The majority of people in Aceh have not benefited from international aid. The practices of intimidation, corruption, and illegal taxation by ex-combatants continue, and some evidence suggests that they have increased (Aspinall 2009).

Notes

1. The Darul Islam Rebellion was triggered by orthodox Muslims in West Java and South Sulawesi, who demanded the formation of an Islamic State of Indonesia (Van Dijk 1981). In 1953 the Rebellion was joined by segments of

the Acehnese political and religious elite, especially as the special status given to Aceh in 1949 was abrogated and the province merged into North Sumatra in 1951 (Dexter 2004). These developments revealed that Islamic dogmatic purity and ethnic identity may have driven the struggle, but that money, power, and distributional justice were its crucial causes.

2. This declaration stipulates no linkage at all between religion and the aim to separate Aceh from the Republic of Indonesia (Ross 2003). There is a general misconception that GAM wants to establish an independent Islamic state of Aceh. This misreading is understandable given that the struggle for an independent Aceh first began as a quest for an Islamic state and that the GoI fomented this perception as a "propaganda ploy to deviate public opinion from the real issue of the conflict" (Kingsbury 2007, 166). Nevertheless, some splinter groups emerged out of the dissatisfaction with GAM's secular orientation; these include the *Front Mujahidin Islam Aceh* (FMIA) in 2001 and *Republik Islam Aceh* (RIA) (Kassim 2006).

3. The transmigration of Javanese to Indonesia's outer islands (*transmigrasi*) was an initiative by the GoI intended to alleviate the problem of overpopulation in Java.

4. The Henry Dunant Centre has since renamed the Centre for Humanitarian Dialogue, referred to as HD Centre.

5. Many people were only temporarily displaced, and by the time the earthquake and tsunami struck Aceh, the provincial government of Aceh reported that only 1,874 people were still officially displaced and living in camps (IOM 2004). This official figure, however, does not account for displaced people living in exile, or with friends and relatives in "safer" urban areas (Mahdi 2006).

6. See, for example, GAM on ASNLF (n.d.); human rights groups such as Koalisi NGO HAM Aceh (n.d.); or the local monthly magazine *Acehkita* (n.d.).

7. Both the Wahid and Megawati governments had remained dependent on the TNI to ensure their political survival. It, in turn, had economic incentives in the perpetuation of the conflict, hence the GoI's lack of interest and will to resolve the Aceh issue once and for all (Aguswandi 2004a). The international community was complacent, and HDC was inexperienced in Aceh. Local and national civil society became marginalized during these peace talks (Aguswandi 2004a; Schulze 2004). GAM and the GoI refused to reexamine their positions (Schulze 2004), and peace efforts were undermined by suspicion and mistrust (Prasodjo and Hamid 2005; Aspinall and Crouch 2003).

8. As coordinating minister of politics and security under Megawati, Yudhoyono functioned as the head of the Aceh Desk created in 2001 to consolidate government policies in Aceh. Yudhoyono opposed Megawati's threats to declare a state of emergency and supported an opening up to foreigners, including election monitors, before being ousted (Neuwirth et al. 2006).

9. This is the result of the second round of the elections, a ballot with former president Megawati. Since Yudhoyono received only 24% of the vote in

the first round (Mahdi 2004), support in Aceh mostly reflected a rejection of Megawati (Aguswandi 2004b).

10. The Centre for an Aceh Referendum (SIRA) was originally mainly composed of students who were demanding a referendum on the political status of Aceh within Indonesia (independence) following the fall of Suharto. Although it has avoided being perceived as such, SIRA was very close to GAM. SIRA retained its acronym but changed its content when it formed its own local political party, "the Independent Voice of the Acehnese People" (*Suara Independen Rakyat* [SIRA]).

11. "PA parliamentarians will now face a similar set of pressures to distribute benefits to those who ensured their victory while also trying to pursue their political agenda. They may also face resistance from pre-existing patronage networks that no longer have access to government largesse. Furthermore, local PA cadres wanting to distribute patronage benefits may come into conflict with the party's top leaders, who are more eager to demonstrate improved governance in Aceh. Concessions to pressure for patronage may guarantee continued peace in the short term, but governance reform has the potential to sustain and consolidate peace in Aceh's new representative democracy well beyond PA's current five-year term" (CPCRS 2009b, 4). "However, the main source of pressure on these new executives thus far has arguably been from GAM's grassroots, contributing to many of the documented conflicts from 2007 until early 2009. Now that a lot more former GAM leaders have gained political office as parliamentarians through the legislative elections, conflicts internal to the organization that were once expressed through violence may now transform into administrative disputes worked out through local governance procedures. In this context, an increase in administrative disputes at the expense of violence and other forms of conflict would be a welcome next step in Aceh's ongoing transition to peace" (2009b, 6).

12. See also Gaillard, Clavé, and Kelman (2008).

13. Rather than a totally new initiative, the 2005 negotiations followed on secret talks initiated during the previous year by Jusuf Kalla. Following agreements for further talks between GoI and GAM negotiators, Martti Ahtisaari was invited by Kalla and Finnish businessman Juha Christensen to facilitate the negotiations four days before the tsunami struck Aceh (Merikallio 2005; *Modus* 2005). A former Finnish president and the chairman of the Finnish NGO Crisis Management Initiative (CMI), Martti Ahtisaari received the approval of the Sweden-based GAM leadership for mediating and invited the two parties to Helsinki (ICG 2005a, 2005b; *Tempo* 2005).

14. The KPA is the civil organization representing former combatants of GAM's military wing, the National Army of Aceh (*Tentara Nasional Aceh* [TNA]).

15. Muzakkir Manaf—the former top commander of the TNA and now head of both the KPA and the local GAM Party, *Partai Aceh*—is also the CEO

and founder of the Pulo Gadeng Group, one of the most important companies and umbrella organizations for business in post-tsunami reconstruction. See Aditjondro 2007.

16. Consequently, two major reintegration-related problems led to confusion, delays, and deep frustration among potential beneficiaries. The first was that the number of GAM fighters was grossly underestimated as a strategic move by GAM to conceal the full extent of its support and to minimize the number of weapons they would have to surrender (Renner 2006b). Furthermore, GAM non-combatants (such as logistics and coordination) were not included as part of the beneficiary group for reintegration funds at all. The second was the conscious avoidance by the GoI of naming the anti-separatist militias as combatant groups to be disarmed, demobilized, and reintegrated (Avonius 2007). Although approximately 15,000 GAM fighters existed at the time the MoU was signed (Aceh interview #101, 2007), according to MoU stipulations GoI reintegration funds could be to only 3,000. The final share in immediate social security benefits for each combatant was only about one-fifth of what each was officially entitled to receive. Many former GAM noncombatants felt excluded altogether until, after long negotiations, 6,200 of them were included in the BRA beneficiary structure by the end of 2006. As for the TNI-backed militias, they, too, were included in the BRA beneficiary structure in May 2006, leading to the withdrawal of GAM and civil society representatives from the BRA (Schulze 2007; ICG 2007).

17. Insecurity and tensions also have other root causes: law enforcement and security sector reform are not well implemented, many illegal weapons are still in circulation, and criminal gangs from outside of Aceh have begun operating in the province.

18. They included, inter alia, the International Committee of the Red Cross, the UN Resident Coordinator's Office, the Indonesian Red Cross, Catholic Relief Services, the World Bank, the International Rescue Committee, and the Dutch organization Humanist Institute for Cooperation With Developing Countries (Zeccola, forthcoming).

19. One interviewee reported that the aid agencies and donor agencies that broadened their target group to include persons affected by the conflict included—among a few others—the International Organization for Migration, the European Commission Humanitarian Aid Office, *Médecins Sans Frontières*, the Canadian International Development Agency, the UN Development Programme, the US Agency for International Development, Caritas, Premier Urgent, Cardi, and the Kreditanstalt für Wiederaufbau. A few others followed later that year. More organizations followed suit in 2007 and 2008.

20. See also BRR and Partners 2008. The authors of this study were well aware that they might seem like potential funders of a credit program; to avoid confusion, they clarified that they were researchers. Still, findings may be skewed if respondents perceived prospects of aid. The fact remains, however, that none

of the fourteen men had full-time work. The situation of the rank-and-file GAM contrasts sharply with GAM who are in political or economic power.

21. The number of local conflicts averaged 100 per month in 2007, as compared to less than 20 in the six months before and after the signing of the MoU. In 2007 the peak was reached in March, with 140 local conflicts per month (World Bank/DSF 2007b). Numbers remain high: in April 2008 this peak was reached again with 144 recorded local-level conflicts, and in May and June 2008 new record highs of 149 and 166 local-level conflicts were reported (World Bank/DSF 2008a; 2008b).

22. Reported incidents of these types of crime have generally increased since the signing of the MoU. Compared to the twenty-two months preceding the signing of the MoU, the crime rate increased fivefold in the twenty-two-month period after the signing (*Serambi* 2008a).

23. Most of the incidents of crime, including robberies, kidnappings, and extortion, are concentrated on the east coast, particularly in the districts of Aceh Utara and Aceh Timur. From December 2007 to April 2008, for example, 50% of the incidents of violence occurred in these districts, including the cities of Lhokseumawe and Langsa (World Bank/DSF 2008a). Both districts have a history of one of the highest levels of GAM–GoI conflict intensity (World Bank 2007). Aceh Timur is the district with the highest poverty level in Aceh (BRR and Partners 2008). Tsunami aid did not change this situation, as the coasts in this district were hardly affected by the tsunami disaster (HIC and OCHA 2005).

24. This term is derived from the Dutch word for "free man" (Ryter 2000).

25. The GoI promised to allocate $20 million in 2005, $60 million in 2006, and $70 million in 2007 to the BRA (ICG 2007). By August 2007 the BRA had allocated $150 million to assist targeted groups. By then, it has disbursed IDR 25 million (around $3,500) to each of the 3,000 GAM combatants, IDR 10 million (around $1,400) to each of the 6,200 GAM noncombatants, IDR 10 million (around $1,400) to each of the 2,035 political prisoners, IDR 5 million (around $700) to each of the 3,024 GAM members who surrendered before the MoU was signed, and IDR 10 million (around $1,400) to 6,500 members of anti-separatist groups (Rayan 2007).

26. See also Ahtisaari, quoted in *Antara* 2008, 1.

7

Conclusion

Humanitarian disasters are inevitable; they will continue to happen. Some will be environmentally induced emergencies that overlap with extant conflicts, creating dual disasters. I thus opt to end this book with a coda rather than a conclusion. Dual disasters can open up new possibilities for diplomacy, inclusion, and innovation, but can also foster disparities, exploitation, and potential neglect.

When humanitarian emergencies intersect as dual disasters, both situations rarely get the same attention. The 2004 tsunami was perhaps the most visually dramatic environmental disaster ever witnessed, and because it was observed globally, it touched many people on many continents. Funding levels were unprecedented, yet money for post-tsunami rehabilitation and reconstruction barely acknowledged the presence of ongoing civil wars in places like Aceh and Sri Lanka.

The tsunami that struck Aceh's coastline accelerated peace talks and helped catalyze the Memorandum of Understanding forged in 2005 that officially marked the end of conflict. Yet, as Chapter 6 illustrated, the spoils of peace were modest for demobilized GAM foot soldiers and their families, as well as for civilian households that had lost homes and jobs during the conflict. Far bigger was the wave of tsunami aid that brought unprecedented international exposure and funds to Aceh.

In Sri Lanka, a related but distinct story from that in Aceh can be told about those displaced and dispossessed by conflict as compared to those affected by the tsunami. IDPs who were uprooted by war but not affected by the tsunami received little, if any, aid when the wave of tsunami aid arrived in Sri Lanka. From the outset, this was a source of tension among IDPs. One of the international donors interviewed stated that his agency maintained a balanced program, ensuring that funding went out to all affected parts of the country (Sri Lanka interview #103, 2007). Such geographical distributions crossed political lines, from areas controlled by the LTTE to those held by government troops. They did not, however, translate into equitable expressions of assistance across the categories of "war-displaced" versus "tsunami-displaced."

Disparities in the Sri Lankan Context

With most humanitarian aid in 2005 earmarked for the tsunami-affected survivors, war-displaced people in Puttalam, Mannar, and the Anuradhapura areas of Sri Lanka's West and Northwest saw little change in their situation. Most of the people in these areas are Sri Lankan Muslims who had fled the east coast and northern Wanni area after the 1990 killings of Muslims at Katankudi and Eravur. By the time the tsunami hit, they had been displaced and dispossessed of their land and homes for more than fifteen years. While the obvious humanitarian needs of those who survived the tsunami were legitimate, the humanitarian crisis created by a longstanding war appeared to be less visible and less urgent in the minds of donors. The neglect of these IDPs did not fuel the conflict in Sri Lanka, but it makes reconciliation an even more pressing challenge now that military conflict is over.

The IDPs in Puttalam who fled their homes in 1990 have been receiving government rations in their temporary homes in the Western Province since their arrival there (Brun 2008). They are the forgotten IDPs, the old caseload of people displaced by war, as it were. They are referred to and often call themselves "refugees" in the Sri Lankan context. Humanitarian aid may be earmarked for specific crises, but every effort must be made to ensure sufficient flexibility in the terms of its provision so as not to increase inequalities, tensions, or resentment among those displaced by humanitarian crises. Humanitarian aid has been and can be incorporated into the fabric of political violence.

Not only were war-displaced people neglected in comparison to tsunami-displaced persons, but the distribution of tsunami aid was itself geographically uneven. Certain politically charged locations attracted disproportionate international attention and resources. The concentration of aid in constituencies represented by senior government ministers was most unfortunate. One aid official we interviewed cited Hambantota, a city on Sri Lanka's southern coast, as a place that received far more than its share of aid: "In comparison to what the North and the East received, more funds went out to the South, especially Hambantota area" (Sri Lanka interview #105, 2007). In December 2005, less than a year after the tsunami, the *Sunday Times* (of London) reported that aid agencies were constructing 4,478 houses in Hambantota, even though only 2,445 were needed (Nelson 2005). Hambantota is the political constituency represented by then prime minister, now president, Mahinda Rajapaksa.

At the same time, in the predominantly Tamil district of Ampara in Sri Lanka's southeastern region, only 3,136 houses had been built for the 18,800 families whose homes were destroyed (Nelson 2005). There is little question that politics distorted aid distributions. In contrast to Aceh, however, the inequities and corruption did not appear to fuel the conflict directly.

The challenge in Sri Lanka is reconciliation. What does reconciliation mean in a post-conflict country where Sinhala triumphalism prevails, Tamil nationalism persists, and violence continues? The Muslims in Puttalam remain displaced; they will want to repossess their lost land and houses or receive government compensation to restore their original homes now that the military conflict is over. Yet two decades have passed since their displacement. Restitution will not be easy.

Tamil people from across Sri Lanka have lost the most. They, too, have forfeited homes and property, much of which has been damaged or destroyed in their absence. Even during the ceasefire, rebuilt tsunami homes were destroyed by fighting along the east coast. As M. de Alwis and Hedman (2009) write,

> An undeclared war thus reigned from around August 2006 until the GoSL formally declared the Ceasefire Agreement null and void, on

January 2, 2008. During this period, the GoSL, with the support
of the Karuna faction, began a systematic operation to rout the
LTTE from the Eastern Province, finally declaring victory on July 18,
2007. Over 150,000 people, primarily Tamils and Muslims, were displaced with many having to flee their newly rebuilt tsunami houses,
scores of which were seriously damaged by shelling and aerial bom-
bardment. (16)

In August 2008 the government of Sri Lanka set the task of routing the
LTTE from the Northern Province at what is now known to be a very
heavy human cost.

In April and May 2009 thousands of unarmed people were caught
in the middle, used as human shields in the vicious fighting between
government troops and the rebels, and killed with impunity. In the
hardest-hit parts of the Northeast, people have seen few signs that their
prospects will improve, in terms of representation, security, or prosperity, save the improved roads along the East Coast and in Jaffna. The political, economic, and social place of Tamil peoples in the fabric of Sri
Lankan society remains unclear.

In May 2010 Sri Lankan President Rajapaksa appointed an eight-
member reconciliation commission of academics and professionals to
examine the issues and circumstances that led to the escalation of the
ethnic separatist armed conflict since 2002. This national response can
be seen as a broad effort to audit the last eight years of war and stave off
an international inquiry. In June 2010, however, at the behest of UN
Secretary General Bai Ki-moon, the United Nations set up its own panel
as part of an accountability process to address potential violations of international humanitarian and human rights law following the violent
end to the civil war in 2009.

By July 2010 the United Nations had closed its office in Colombo,
due to a public protest of the UN inquiry led by Sri Lanka's construction minister, Wimal Weerawansa, an ally of the president. Mr. Ban said
it was unacceptable that Sri Lankan authorities had failed to prevent the
disruption of work by UN staff (Reuters 2010). In the same month, the
Sri Lankan government faced a blow to its economy when the European
Union halted preferential treatment for Sri Lankan imports, citing its
lack of commitment to resolving human rights complaints (Bajaj 2010).
Sri Lanka will lose the GSP (Generalized System of Preferences) plus

trading status, which means that higher tariffs will apply to its exports; the cost will be roughly $1.56 billion annually.

Just as the devolution of governance and political change proceed in Aceh, Sri Lanka has a long way to go before reconciliation and social inclusion of all constituencies are achieved. In Sri Lanka, no peace was ever forged. A sense of justice and fairness is prerequisite to any bona fide peace. This will be difficult to achieve, given the dramatic loss of life among Tamils in the North and East, and the recalcitrance of the Sri Lankan government to address this loss.

Conflict Tsunamis:
New Spaces, Persistent Challenges

The tsunami opened up new political spaces for negotiation, known as "disaster diplomacy" (Kelman and Gaillard 2007). The utter destruction and dramatic loss of life in Aceh accelerated peace talks, and the Memorandum of Understanding securing the end of conflict was signed in August 2005. But the tsunami also opened up another order of political space in Aceh: international access to the region. Until the devastation of the tsunami, most foreigners were not allowed in Aceh. The tsunami rendered Aceh visible to the outside world, and its conflict, experience of human rights violations, and struggles slowly registered with faraway publics that did not otherwise follow Indonesian politics.

In Sri Lanka the tsunami had a different political valence. Both the eastern coastline and southern shores of the country were deeply affected, and all of the country's ethnic groups were represented among the lives lost and the survivors. But government responses to the tsunami in the Sinhala-dominated South were seen as more permissive and beneficial to survivors there than those in the East, where more Tamil and Muslim communities are situated. The example of the buffer zones outlined in Chapters 2 and 3 illustrates how policies, ostensibly made in the name of public safety after a disaster, can actually reignite tensions that have fueled competing nationalisms and war in Sri Lanka since 1983.

On a more positive note, the tsunami has created new social relations and opened up societal space for people who lost family members in the tsunami. While preliminary in scope, the research presented in

Chapter 4 shows how remarriage for tsunami widows and widowers is possible if not always desirable, given potential consequences for children. Whereas war widows rarely remarried before the tsunami, they, too, witnessed change and openings after the tsunami at the very visceral intersection of dual disasters. The stigma of being widowed remains, but the options for women who lost their spouses in the tsunami have increased.

Disaster Capitalism: New Spaces to Profit

> It is apparent that allocation and programming, particularly in the first weeks and months of 2005, were driven by the extent of public and media interest, and by the unprecedented funding available, rather than by assessment and need. A real system of decision making based on humanitarian principles was lacking. Much of the implementation response was driven by the availability of funds, or by contextual opportunism, rather than by needs. (TEC 2006, 8)

Too much money provided too quickly without the capacity or oversight to spend accountably is a recipe for a disaster of another sort. While much was accomplished in terms of reconstruction, mistakes were also made.

In March 2010 the Canadian Broadcasting Corporation (CBC) ran an exclusive feature on post-tsunami aid in Aceh. The story traced the outsourcing of work to rebuild homes destroyed in the tsunami by humanitarian agencies that did not have the capacity to undertake and oversee the reconstruction themselves. Thousands of Javanese migrant workers were brought to Aceh by Indonesian contractors to build new homes. Virgil Grandfield (2010) was employed by an international humanitarian agency after the tsunami and later wrote a report based on the migrants' experiences. Many were never paid for their work and experienced ongoing hunger on the job. Contractors promised daily meals and decent pay, but Grandfield (2010) documents hundreds of cases where these terms were not met.

> Approximately 75 per cent of over 1,000 tsunami workers discovered by investigators in Java described experiences of false recruitment, extremely low or periods of non-payment and involuntary labour on sites because of deception by mandors [contractors], no money to purchase transportation, and/or geographic isolation. (8)

Javanese workers were cheaper to employ than locals, and some 200,000 of these migrants were brought in to provide a workforce not even available in Aceh. Mandors, or contractors, sought to make money off the agreements signed with INGOs such as the Canadian Red Cross. Hence, the ways in which this labor was secured were contrary to humanitarian principles and to the intent of many donors, whose funds made reconstruction possible.

One might point to this travesty as the perfect example of Naomi Klein's (2007) disaster capitalism thesis: disasters spawn business opportunities and actors that seek to maximize profit in moments and spaces of vulnerability. Yet I contend that this egregious lack of oversight, a claim subsequently refuted by the Canadian Red Cross, was as much an expression of humanitarian hubris as an illustration of capricious capitalism. Never before did humanitarian agencies receive so much money to address an emergency, namely the damage and loss of the 2004 tsunami. For many, the capacity to spend these funds accountably, using direct project management as their approach, was almost impossible.

MSF actually stopped taking donations when it met its assessed needs for funding, an act unthinkable at the time, but one that was very wise in retrospect. Whether or not multinational hotel chains buy and develop sleepy surfing beaches in Sri Lanka's Southeast, as Klein (2007) predicts, remains to be seen. New forms of post-conflict, post-tsunami property speculation are certainly under way.[1] Yet disaster capitalism must be situated among other dynamic political processes at work: disaster nationalism, disaster diplomacy, disaster distrust.

Competition among humanitarian actors was also a problem (TEC 2006), and most evaluations admit that coordination could have been better (Cosgrave 2007). Small steps have been made. A funding appeal made after the Haiti earthquake in 2010 demonstrated more cooperation among humanitarian actors who might otherwise be competing for the same donor dollars. In Canada, private citizens had an opportunity to donate to the Humanitarian Coalition, a group of four Canadian NGOs that operate internationally and that would normally collect donations individually.[2] This kind of cooperation is a first step toward a more coordinated INGO sector, one hopefully less likely to fall prey to humanitarian hubris.

Dual Disasters on the Rise

What will be the next set of dual disasters? And where? Some humanitarian crises are not even afforded the modest analysis presented here due to state secrecy and restricted access to international researchers. Burma (aka Myanmar) has been a bastion of state repression and human rights violations since 1988 when the military junta killed many participants in a peaceful protest. Hardly a word was heard about the impact of the tsunami in Burma, and yet its proximity to Thailand suggests that it was very adversely affected. Such state policies of secrecy and isolationism are themselves disastrous, precluding emergency aid for affected civilians.

Fine-tuning disaster aid so that it is conflict sensitive has also been identified as critical in the context of dual disasters. If humanitarian assistance after an earthquake unwittingly fuels an extant conflict in the area, it fails. Above all, "do no harm" (Anderson 1999). Technical expertise in emergency relief operations is critical, but must be complemented by knowledge of politics, culture, and livelihoods, so that the social, economic, and political landscapes that precede disaster can be figured into humanitarian responses. And as professional standards increase among emergency aid actors and practices improve, "Humanitarians are much better at saving lives than they used to be" (de Waal 2010, S130).

> The technical proficiency and material resources of the humanitarian
> enterprise mitigate much needless suffering, but they are never enough
> to fulfil the rights of victims and survivors. (de Waal 2010, S130)

Political will and cultural resources are just as important as technical fixes in humanitarian crises.

With the summer of 2010 recorded as one of the hottest in history,[3] the effects of global warming are increasing sea temperatures and sea levels, which scientists correlate with a greater number of extreme weather events in the years to come (Geist et al. 2006; Gore 2006). Where they intersect with war or other humanitarian emergencies, the responsibilities of those delivering aid become even more onerous. Learning from the 2004 tsunami and from the 2010 earthquake that hit an already precarious Haiti is crucial to creating more accountable and responsive humanitarian action.

Notes

1. I am grateful to Jessi Lehman for her research assistance in Sri Lanka on political conditions and post-tsunami projects in the Eastern Province in 2009. She found that twenty-nine foreign investors had a stake in Passikudah beach development, north of Batticaloa. Nonetheless, the beach remained largely undeveloped at the time of our visit in June 2009, save one small guest house.

2. Oxfam Canada, Oxfam Quebec, Save the Children Canada, and Care Canada were all part of the Humanitarian Coalition funding appeal after the Haitian earthquake in January 2010.

3. The *Globe and Mail* reported that throughout Canada, the heat has been far more pronounced than the global average. Temperatures from January 2010 onward were, at the time of this writing, 3.9 degrees above average, shattering the previous record of 3.2 degrees set in 2006. The US National Oceanic and Atmospheric Administration confirmed that the Earth was on course for the hottest year since record-keeping began in 1880, running 0.7 degrees (Celsius) above the twentieth-century average.

Bibliography

Every effort has been made to ensure that the URLs in this book are accurate and up-to-date. However, with the rapid changes that occur in the World Wide Web, it is inevitable that some pages or other resources will have been discontinued or moved, and some content modified or reorganized. The publisher recommends that readers who cannot find the sources or information they seek with the URLs in this book use one of the numerous search engines available on the Internet.

Publications

Abeysekera, Charles, and Newton Gunasinghe, eds. 1987. *Facets of ethnicity in Sri Lanka*. Colombo: Social Scientists Association.

Accra Agenda for Action. 2008. Third high level forum on aid effectiveness. Accessed March 10, 2010, at http://www.undp.org/mdtf/docs/Accra-Agenda-for-Action.pdf.

AMM (Aceh Monitoring Mission). n.d. Aceh Monitoring Mission website. http://www.aceh-mm.org/english/amm_menu/about.htm.

Acehkita. n.d. Website. http://www.acehkita.com.

Aditjondro, G.J. 2007. Profiting from peace: The political economy of Aceh's post-Helsinki reconstruction. Working Paper 3. Brussels: International NGO Forum on Indonesian Development.

Agamben, Giorgio. 1998. *Homo sacer: Sovereign power and bare life*. Trans. D. Heller-Roazen. Stanford, CA: Stanford University Press.

Agglomerations 2001 Census. 20% Sample Data Cat. No. 97F0009XCB01002.

Aguswandi. 2004a. *Searching for peace in Asia Pacific: An overview of conflict prevention and peace-building activities.* Boulder, CO: Lynne Rienner Publishers.

———. 2004b. Aceh: A testing ground for Susilo's promises. *Jakarta Post.* November 1.

ALNAP (Active Learning Network for Accountability and Performance in Humanitarian Action). 2009. Website. Accessed on December 1, 2010 at http://www.alnap.org/initiatives/tec.aspx.

Amoore, Louise. 2006. Biometric borders: Governing mobilities in the war on terror. *Political Geography* 25: 336–51.

———, and Marieke de Goede. 2005. Governance, risk and dataveillance in the war on terror. *Crime, Law and Social Change* 43: 149–73.

Anderson, Mary B. 1999. *Do no harm: How aid can support peace—or war.* Boulder, CO: Lynne Rienner.

Antara. 2008. Reintegration of former GAM members into society remains difficult: Ahtassari. May 7.

Apps, Peter. 2006. Shelling a call to war, Tamil rebels say. *Globe and Mail,* August 7.

Asian Coalition for Housing Rights. Website. Accessed February 10, 2008, at http://www.achr.net (tsunami links to both Indonesia and Sri Lanka can be found here).

Askandar, K. 2006. *The Aceh conflict and the roles of the civil society.* Banda Aceh: Aceh Institute.

ASNLF (Aceh/Sumatra National Liberation Front). n.d. Website. http://www.asnlf.net/.

Aspinall, Edward. 2007. Guerillas in power. *Inside Indonesia.*

———. 2008. Basket case to showcase: How Indonesia's democratic transition transformed Aceh. *Inside Indonesia* 92, April/June.

———. 2009. *Islam and nation: Separatist rebellion in Aceh, Indonesia.* Stanford, CA: Stanford University Press.

———, and H. Crouch. 2003. The Aceh peace process: Why it failed. *Policy Studies* 1. Washington DC: East–West Center.

Associated Press. 2005. Report: Sri Lankan president pushes for controversial buffer zone after tsunami scare. March 29.

———. 2008. Police investigate deadly attack on ex-rebels in Aceh. March 3.

———. 2010. Haiti promised €230m as Nicolas Sarkozy visits former colony: French president cancels island's debt and acknowledges wounds of France's brutal colonization. *The Guardian,* February 17.

Avonius, L. 2007. Perceptions and practices of reintegration in Aceh. Unpublished Conference Paper. EuroSEAS Conference. Naples.

Awaludin, H., and M. Mahmud. 2005. Memorandum of Understanding between the Government of the Republic of Indonesia and the Free Aceh Movement. Accessed May 12, 2010, at http://www.aceh-mm.org/download/english/Helsinki%20MoU.pdf.

Bagwe, Anjali. 1998. *Of woman caste.* London: Zed Books.

Bajaj, Vikas. 2010. Sri Lanka loses E.U. trade benefit. *New York Times,* July 6.

Bajak, F. 2010. Why Chile dodged Haiti-style ruin. Associated Press. In *Toronto Star,* February 28.

Barter, Shane J. 2004. Holy war or open door? The role of Islam in the Aceh conflict. CANCAPS Conference, Quebec City, Quebec.

Bastian, Sunil. 2007a. Globalisation, foreign aid and conflict—the case of Sri Lanka. Occasional paper. *Law & Society Trust Review,* July 25.

———. 2007b. *The politics of foreign aid in Sri Lanka.* Colombo: International Centre for Ethnic Studies.

Bauman, Zygmunt. 1998. *Globalization: The human consequences.* Oxford: Polity.

Beek, C. 2007. *Re-paving the road to peace: Analysis of the implementation of DD&R in Aceh province, Indonesia.* BICC Brief 35. Bonn: BICC.

Bigo, Didier. 2002. Security and immigration: Toward a critique of the governmentality of unease. *Alternatives* 27: 63–92.

Booth, W., and S. Wilson. 2010. Destruction of schools in Haiti quake crushes hopes of a better future for many. *Washington Post,* January 23. Accessed January 25, 2010, at http://www.washingtonpost.com/wp-dyn/content/article/2010/01/22/AR2010012203476.html?hpid=artslot&sid=ST2010012101758.

Boyce, J. 2002. Unpacking aid. *Development and Change* 33: 239–46.

Braun, B. 2005. Writing geographies of hope. *Antipode* 37: 834–41.

BRR and Partners. 2005. *Aceh and Nias one year after the tsunami: The recovery effort and way forward.* Washington DC: Badan Rehabilitasi dan Rekonstruksi/World Bank.

———. 2008. *The impact of the conflict, the tsunami and reconstruction on poverty in Aceh: Aceh poverty assessment 2008.* Washington DC: Badan Rehabilitasi dan Rekonstruksi/World Bank.

Brun, Cathrine. 2008. *Finding a place: Local integration and protracted displacement in Sri Lanka.* Colombo: Social Scientists Association.

Burnside, C., and D. Dollar. 1997. Aid policies and growth. Policy Research Working Paper 1777. Washington DC: World Bank.

———. 2000. Aid, policies, and growth. *American Economic Review* 90: 847–68.

———. 2004. Aid, policies, and growth: Revisiting the evidence. World Bank Policy Research Paper 3251.

Cameron, R. 2004. (Senior Vice President, CIDA) Address to stakeholders in Vancouver. November 25. Wosk Centre, Simon Fraser University.

Cassidy, J. 2002. Helping hands: How foreign aid could benefit everybody. *New Yorker,* March 18, 60–66.

Cassim, Nisthar. 2005. Government gets flexible on buffer zone rule. *Daily Mirror,* October 10.

CCR (Canadian Council for Refugees). 2010. Guaranteeing life, liberty, security and humanity for refugees in Canada—25 years after Singh. Accessed at www.ccrweb.ca/RRday.htm.

Centre for Policy Alternatives. 2005. Landlessness and land rights in post-tsunami Sri Lanka. Commissioned by International Federation of the Red Cross, Colombo. November 16.

Chattopadhyay, R. 2002. A new peace initiative in Sri Lanka. *Forum of Federations.* Accessed July 8, 2008, at http://www.forumfed.org/en/libdocs/Federations/V2N5-lk-Chattopadhyay.pdf.

Cheran, Rudhramoorthy. 2000. *Changing formations: Tamil nationalism and national liberation in Sri Lanka and the diaspora.* Ph.D. dissertation. Toronto: York University.

Choi, Vivian. 2009. A safer Sri Lanka? Technology, security and preparedness in post-tsunami Sri Lanka. In *Tsunami in a time of war: Aid, activism and reconstruction in Sri Lanka and Aceh,* 191–215. Ed. M. de Alwis and E.-L. Hedman. Colombo: International Centre for Ethnic Studies.

Chung, A. 2010. How to mend a "broken" nation. *Toronto Star,* February 20.

CIC (Citizenship and Immigration Canada). 2001. Facts and figures 2000: Immigration overview. Ottawa: Ministry of Public Works and Government Services Canada.

CIDA (Canadian International Development Agency). 2001. Strengthening aid effectiveness: New approaches to Canada's international assistance program. Consultation document. February 16. Shorter version published June 2001.

———. 2002. Canada making a difference in the world: A policy statement on strengthening aid effectiveness. Minister of Public Works and Government Services, Hull, Canada. September. Accessed July 28, 2008, at http://www.acdi-cida.gc.ca/cidaweb/acdicida.nsf/En/STE-32015515-SG4.

———. 2003. Program in Sri Lanka: An overview. 2nd edition. August. (No publication information.)

———. 2005a. CIDA announces new development partners: Developing countries where Canada can make a difference. News release. April 19. Accessed July 28, 2006, at http://www.acdi-cida.gc.ca/cidaweb/acdicida.nsf/En/JER-324115437-MU7.

———. 2005b. A role of pride and influence in the world: Development, Canada's international policy statement. Gatineau, QC: Her Majesty the Queen in Right of Canada.

————. 2009. Increased aid volumes and effectiveness. Accessed March 22, 2010, at http://www.acdicida.gc.ca/acdi-cida/ACDI-CIDA.nsf/eng/JUD-1318137-HHX.

Clark, Nigel. 2007. Living through the tsunami: Vulnerability and generosity on a volatile earth. *Geoforum* 38(6): 1127–39.

Cockburn, Cynthia. 1998. *The space between us: Negotiating gender and national identities in conflict.* London: Zed Press.

Collier, Paul, Anke Hoeffler, and Mans Soderboom. 2006. Post-conflict risks. Working Paper No. 256. Oxford: Centre for the Study of African Economics, University of Oxford.

Connelly, William. 2002. *Neuropolitics: Thinking, culture, speed.* Minneapolis: University of Minnesota Press.

Cosgrave, J. 2007. Synthesis report: Expanded summary—joint evaluation of the international response to the Indian Ocean tsunami. London: Tsunami Evaluation Coalition. Accessed February 21, 2010, at http://www.alnap.org/initiatives/tec.aspx.

Couldrey, Marion, and Tim Morris. 2005. UN assesses tsunami response. *Forced Migration Review.* Special issue (tsunami) 24: 6–9.

CPCRS (Center for Peace and Conflict Resolution Studies). 2009a. Aceh Peace Monitoring Update 1 March–30 June 2009. Syiah Kuala University, Banda Aceh.

————. 2009b. Aceh Peace Monitoring Update 1 July–31 August 2009. Syiah Kuala University, Banda Aceh.

Culbert, Vance. 2005. Civil society development vs. the peace dividend: International aid in the Wanni. *Disasters* 29(1): 38–57.

Dahlman, Carl T. 2009. Post-conflict. In *Key concepts in political geography,* 235–46. Los Angeles: Sage.

Daniel, Val. 1997. Suffering nation and alienation. In *Social suffering,* 309–58. Ed. A. Kleinman, V. Das, and M. Lock. Berkeley: University of California Press.

Danner, M. 2010. To heal Haiti, look to history, not nature. *New York Times,* January 21. Accessed January 23, 2010, at http://www.nytimes.com/2010/01/22/opinion/22danner.html?scp=1&sq=danner&st=cse.

de Alwis, Kingsley A. 2005. The 100-metre rule—what's the logic? *The Island,* May 25.

de Alwis, Malathi. 1998. Moral mothers and stalwart sons. In *Women and war reader,* 254–71. Ed. Lois Ann Lorentzen and Jennifer Turpin. New York: New York University Press.

————. 2009. A double wounding? Aid and activism in post-tsunami Sri Lanka. In *Tsunami in a time of war: Aid, activism and reconstruction in Sri*

Lanka and Aceh, 121–38. Ed. M. de Alwis and E.-L. Hedman. Colombo: International Centre for Ethnic Studies.

———, and Eva-Lotta Hedman. 2009. Introduction. In *Tsunami in a time of war: Aid, activism and reconstruction in Sri Lanka and Aceh,* 9–27. Ed. M. de Alwis and E.-L. Hedman. Colombo: International Centre for Ethnic Studies.

de Alwis, Malathi, and Jennifer Hyndman. 2002. *Capacity-building in conflict zones: A feminist analysis of humanitarian assistance in Sri Lanka.* Colombo: International Centre for Ethnic Studies.

de Mel, Neloufer, and Kanchana N. Ruwanpura. 2006. *Gendering the tsunami: Women's experiences from Sri Lanka.* Report Series. Colombo: International Centre for Ethnic Studies.

de Waal, Alex. 2010. The humanitarians' tragedy: Escapable and inescapable cruelties. *Disasters* 34(S2): S130–37.

Dexter, P. 2004. *Historical analysis of population reactions to stimuli: A case study of Aceh.* Edinburgh, Australia: Land Operations Division, Defence Science and Technology Organisation.

Dias, Sunimalee. 2006. Key donors divided over post-tsunami work. *Daily Mirror,* February 7.

Diebel, L. 2010. Re-imagining Haiti. *Toronto Star,* January 24.

Dixon, R. 2010. Aristide, Haiti's exiled ex-president, offers to return and help rebuild. *Los Angeles Times,* January 15. Accessed January 25, 2010, at http://www.latimes.com/news/nation-and-world/la-fg-haiti-aristide16-2010jan16,0,6151310.story.

Dow Jones Newswires. 2008. Indonesia agency finds massive potential hydrocarbon reserves. February 14.

Duffield, Mark. 1996. The symphony of the damned: Racial discourse, complex political emergencies and humanitarian aid. *Disasters* 20(3): 173–93.

———. 2001. *Global governance and the new wars: The merging of development and security.* London: Zed Books.

———. 2008. Global civil war: The non-insured, international containment and post-interventionary society. *Journal of Refugee Studies* 21(2): 145–65.

Dugger, Celia. 2005. Trade and aid to poorest seen as crucial on agenda for richest nations. *The New York Times,* June 18.

Easterly, W., R. Levine, and D. Roodman. 2003. New data, new doubts: A comment on Burnside and Dollar's Aid, policies, and growth (2000). Development Research Institute Working Paper Series 4, RR#2003-04. Accessed July 28, 2006, at http://www.nyu.edu/fas/institute/dri/DRIWP/DRIWP04.pdf.

Economist. 2005a. Development: Recasting the case for aid. January 22.

———. 2005b. Relief but little rebuilding. December 24.

———. 2010a. Victory for the tiger-slayer. January 28.

———. 2010b. Lessons from the tsunami: Too much of a good thing? January 23.

Elliott, Carolyn M. 2005. Introduction. In *A space of her own,* 9–19. Ed. Leela Gulati and Jasodhara Bagchi. New Delhi: Thousand Oaks; London: Sage.

Emmanuel, Sarala. 2005. Contextualizing post-tsunami challengers: Research findings of household survey in tsunami-affected areas. Proceedings of South Asian Conference on Gender Concerns in Post-Tsunami Reconstruction. July 15–16. Suriya Women's Development Centre, Batticaloa, Sri Lanka.

Eviatar, D. 2003. Do aid studies govern policies or reflect them? *The New York Times,* July 26.

Farmer, Paul. 1994. *The uses of Haiti.* Monroe, ME: Common Courage Press.

Faul, M. 2010. Sarkozy tells Haiti: "You are not alone." *Toronto Star,* February 18.

Fernando, Santhush. 2005. Sri Lanka to strictly enforce exclusion zone. *Sunday Times,* April 24.

Friedman, M., and R. Friedman. 1982. *Capitalism and freedom.* Chicago: University of Chicago Press.

Fuglerud, Oivind. 1999. *Life on the outside: The Tamil diaspora and long-distance nationalism.* London: Pluto Press.

Gaillard J.-C., E. Clavé, and I. Kelman. 2008. Wave of peace? Tsunami disaster diplomacy in Aceh, Indonesia. *Geoforum* 39(1): 511–26.

Geist, Eric L., Vasily V. Titov, and Costas E. Synolakis. 2006. Tsunami: Wave of change. *Scientific American,* January, 56–65.

Glassman, Jim. 2005. Editorial: Tsunamis and other forces of destruction. *Environment and Planning D: Society and Space* 23: 164–70.

Glenny, Misha. 1992. *The fall of Yugoslavia: The third Balkan war.* London: Penguin.

GoI (Government of Indonesia). 2005. Peraturan Presiden Republik Indonesia Nomor 30 Tahun 2005 tentang Rencana Induk Rehabilitasi dan Rekonstruksi Wilayah dan Kehidupan Masyarakat Provinsi Nanggroe Aceh Darussallam dan Kepulauan Nias Provinsi Sumatera Utara. In Buku Rinci Bidang Ketertiban. *Keamandan dan Ketahanan Masyarakat.* Jakarta: Government of Indonesia.

———. 2006. *Humanitarian coordination: Indonesia's experience in dealing with humanitarian coordination.* Panel Discussion on Disaster Response. New York: Permanent Mission of the Government of Indonesia to the United Nations.

———, and GAM. 2005. Memorandum of Understanding between the Government of the Republic of Indonesia and the Free Aceh Movement. http://www.old.thejakartapost.com/RI_GAM_MOU.pdf.

Good, B., M.-J. DelVecchio Good, J. Grayman, and M. Lakoma. 2006. *Psychosocial needs assessment of communities affected by the conflict in the districts of Pidie, Bireuen, and Aceh Utara.* Geneva: International Organization for Migration.

Gore, Al. 2006. *An inconvenient truth: The planetary emergency of global warming and what we can do about it.* Emmaus, PA: Rodale.

Grandfield, Virgil. 2010. Outsourcing disaster: Human trafficking and humanitarian failure in Aceh's tsunami reconstruction. Briade Cahaya and the Aceh Institute.

Graves, S., and V. Wheeler. 2006. Good humanitarian donorship: Overcoming obstacles to improved collective donor performance. Humanitarian Policy Group discussion paper. December.

Gregory, Derek. 2004. *The colonial present.* Malden, MA: Blackwell.

Grundy-Warr, Carl, and James D. Sidaway. 2006. Political geographies of silence and erasure. *Political Geography* 25: 479–81.

Gunasinghe, Newton. 1987. Ethnic conflict in Sri Lanka: Perceptions and solutions. In *Facets of Ethnicity in Sri Lanka,* 61–71. Colombo: Social Scientists Association.

Hamid, I.A. 2007. Inauguration speech of North Aceh district head Ilyas A. Hamid. March 3. Lhokseumawe.

Hedman, Eva-Lotta. 2005. Introduction. In *Forced Migration Review* special issue (tsunami) 24: 4–5.

HIC and OCHA (Humanitarian Information Centre and Office for the Coordination of Humanitarian Affairs). 2005. Villages directly impacted by the tsunami. Map. Accessed November 20, 2010, at http://www.humanitarian info.org/sumatra/mapcentre/docs/01_General_map/SUM01-001_Aceh_ Disaster_Area_HIC_2005-04-08_A3.pdf.

Hollenbeck, Leroy. 2007. . . . and then there were elections. Now what? Washington DC: USINDO Brief. Accessed December 13, 2007, at http://www .usindo.org/publications/briefs/2007/Hollenbeck010507.pdf.

Honorine, S. 2007. Tsunami's tide of goodwill leaves rebels in the cold. *South China Morning Post,* September 10.

hooks, bell. 2000. *All about love: New visions.* New York: Perennial.

Hoole, R., D. Somasundaram, K. Sritharan, and R. Thiranagama. 1990. *The broken palmyra—the Tamil crisis in Sri Lanka.* Claremont, CA: The Sri Lanka Studies Institute. April. Accessed July 10, 2008, at http://www.uthr .org/BP/Content.htm.

Hout, Will. 2002. Good governance and aid: Selectivity criteria in development assistance. *Development and Change* 33(3): 511–27.

HRW (Human Rights Watch). 2001. *The war in Aceh.* 13. New York: Human Rights Watch.

Hyndman, Jennifer. 1998. Managing difference: Gender and culture in humanitarian emergencies. *Gender, Place, and Culture* 5(3): 241–60.

———. 2003a. Aid, conflict, and migration: The Canada–Sri Lanka connection. *Canadian Geographer* 47(3): 251–68.

———. 2003b. Beyond gender: Towards a feminist analysis of humanitarianism and development in Sri Lanka. *Women's Studies Quarterly* 31(3–4): 212–26.

———. 2003c. Preventive, palliative, or punitive? Safe spaces in Bosnia-Herzegovina, Somalia, and Sri Lanka. *Journal of Refugee Studies* 16(2): 167–85.

———. 2005a. Genocide and ethnic cleansing. In *The gender companion,* 201–11. Ed. D. Goldberg, P. Essed, and A. Kobayashi. Oxford: Blackwell Publishers.

———. 2005b. Migration wars: Refuge or refusal? *Geoforum* 36(1): 3–6.

———. 2006. Gender, space, and security in post-tsunami Sri Lanka. Presentation to the International Association of Studies in Forced Migration. Toronto. June 19.

———. 2007a. The securitization of fear in post-tsunami Sri Lanka. *Annals of the Association of American Geographer* 97(2): 361–72.

———. 2007b. Fear and conflict in post-tsunami Sri Lanka. *Annals of the Association of American Geographers* 97(2): 361–72.

———. In press. Feminist geopolitics revisited: Body counts in Iraq. *Professional Geographer.*

———. Forthcoming. Acts of aid: Neoliberalism in a war zone. *Antipode.*

———, and Mala de Alwis. 2004. Bodies, shrines, and roads: Violence, (im)mobility, and displacement in Sri Lanka. *Gender, Place and Culture* 11(4): 535–57.

———, and Mala de Alwis. 2003. Beyond gender: Towards a feminist analysis of humanitarianism and development in Sri Lanka. *Women's Studies Quarterly* 31 (3–4): 212–26.

ICG (International Crisis Group). 2005a. Aceh: A new chance for peace? *Asia Briefing* 40. Jakarta/Brussels: ICG.

———. 2005b. Aceh: So far, so good. *Asia Briefing* 44. Jakarta/Brussels: ICG.

———. 2007. Aceh: Post-conflict complications. *Asia Report* 137. Jakarta: ICG.

———. 2010. War Crimes in Sri Lanka. *Asia Report* 191, May.

Institute for Policy Studies. 2005. *Sri Lanka: State of the economy 2005.* October. Colombo: Institute for Policy Studies.

IOM (International Organization for Migration). 2004. Update on the IDP situation in Aceh. December 20.

Ismail, Qadri. 1995. Unmooring identity: The antimonies of elite Muslim self-representation in modern Sri Lanka. In *Unmaking the nation: The politics*

of identity and history in modern Sri Lanka, 55–105. Eds. Pradeep Jeganathan and Qadri Ismail. Colombo: Social Scientists Association.

Iyer, P., and C. Mitchell. 2004. *The collapse of peace zones in Aceh.* Research
paper. Fairfax, VA: Institute for Conflict Analysis and Resolution, George
Mason University.

Jakarta Post. 2008. Pertamina may develop gigantic reserve in western shore of
Aceh. February 12.

———. 2010. Hundreds dressed down by sharia officers during raid on clothing. January 26.

Jansz, Frederica. 2005. Using the tsunami to muzzle the people. *Sunday Leader,*
February 20.

Jayawardena, Kumari. 1986. *Feminism and nationalism in the third world.* London: Zed Books.

———. 1990. *Ethnic and class conflicts in Sri Lanka: Some aspects of Sinhala
Buddhist consciousness over the past 100 years.* Colombo: Sanjwa Books.

———, and Malathi de Alwis. 1996. Introduction. In *Embodied violence: Com-
munalising women's sexuality in south Asia,* ix–xxii. Ed. Kumari Jayawardena
and Malathi de Alwis. New Delhi: Kali for Women.

Jeganathan, Pradeep. 2005. South paw one. *Lines* (e-journal) 3(4). Accessed
July 10, 2008, at www.lines-magazine.org/Art_Feb05/Pradeep.htm.

———, and Qadri Ismail. 1995. Introduction: Unmaking the Nation. In *Unmaking the Nation: The Politics of Identity and History in Modern Sri Lanka,*
11–19. Eds. R. Jeganathan and Q. Ismail. Colombo: Social Scientists
Association.

Jeyeraj, D.B.S. 2005. The state that failed its people. *Sunday Leader,* February 6.

Kangararachchi, Ramini, and Irangika Range. 2005. 65 percent of tsunami hit
shun buffer zone. *Daily News,* Colombo, June 2.

Kassim, Y.R. 2006. Post-tsunami GAM and the future of Aceh. *Straits Times,*
February 12.

Kay, K. 2003. The 'new humanitarianism': The Henry Dunant Centre and the
Aceh peace negotiations. Woodrow Wilson School Case Study. February,
at wws.princeton.edu/research/cases/newhumanit.pdf.

Kelly, Philip F. 1999. The geographies and politics of globalization. *Progress in
Human Geography* 23: 379–400.

Kelman, I., and J.-C. Gaillard. 2007. Disaster diplomacy in Aceh. *Humanitarian Exchange: Practice and Policy Notes* 37: 37–39.

Kennedy, J., J. Ashmore, E. Babister, and I. Kelman. 2008. The meaning of
'build back better': Evidence from post-tsunami Aceh and Sri Lanka. *Journal of Contingencies and Crisis Management* 16(1): 24–36.

Kingsbury, D. 2007. The Free Aceh Movement: Islam and democratisation. *Journal of Contemporary Asia* 37(2): 166–89.

Klein, Naomi. 2005. The rise of disaster capitalism. *The Nation,* May 2.

———. 2007. *The shock doctrine: The rise of disaster capitalism.* New York: Metropolitan.

Kleinfeld, M. 2007. Misreading the post-tsunami political landscape in Sri Lanka: The myth of humanitarian space. *Space and Polity* 11(2): 169–84.

Knockaert, J. 2004. Canada making a difference in the world. CIDA presentation and overview. Victoria. June 8.

Koalisi NGO HAM Aceh. n.d. Website. http://www.koalisi-ham.org.

Korf, B. 2005. Sri Lanka: The tsunami after the tsunami. *International Development Planning Review* 27(3): i–vii.

Laksono, D.D. 2005. For the sake of the civilians. *Acehkita,* July 15.

Lawson, Victoria. 2005. Natural disaster or space of vulnerability. *AAG Newsletter* 40(3): 3–4.

Le Billon, Philippe, and Arno Waizenegger. 2007. Peace in the wake of disaster? Secessionist conflicts and the 2004 Indian Ocean tsunami. *Transactions of the Institute of British Geographers* 32(3): 411–27.

Le Blanc, Daniel. 2006. 'We won't win' unless aid money flows. *Globe and Mail,* October 6.

Leckie, Scott. 2005. New housing, land and property restitution rights. *Forced Migration Review* 25: 52–53.

Lindsey, T. 2001. The criminal state: Premanisme and the new Indonesia. In *Indonesia today: Challenges of history,* 283–97. Ed. G. Lloyd and S. Smith. Singapore: ISEAS.

Lovgren, Stefan. 2006. Al Gore's inconvenient truth movie: Fact or hype? *National Geographic News.* Accessed July 9, 2010 at http://news.national geographic.com/news/2006/05/060524-global-warming.html.

MacKinnon, M. 2010. How to fix a broken city. *Globe and Mail,* January 16.

Macrae, Joanna, and Nick Leader. 2000. Shifting sands: The search for "coherence" between political and humanitarian responses to complex emergencies. Humanitarian Policy Group Report 8. London: Overseas Development Institute. August.

Mahdi, Saiful. 2004. *Acehnese giving Susilo another chance.* Banda Aceh: Aceh Institute.

———. 2006. IDPs and poverty problem: Aceh conflict and tsunami IDPs mobility and its spatial statistics. 8th Indonesian Regional Science Association (IRSA) International Conference. University of Brawijaya, Malang,

Indonesia. Accessed November 28, 2010, at www.aceheye.org/data_files/ english...analysis_others_2006_00_00.pdf.

Mahmood, M. 2005. Opening speech to the Helsinki peace talks on February 22, 2005. Accessed November 13, 2007, at http://www.asnlf.net/asnlf_my/ my/asnlf/swedia/pr_asnlf_050223ing.htm.

Mangkusubroto, K. 2009. Reflections on tsunami reconstruction. Excerpt from a speech. Jakarta. January 1. Accessed May 14, 2010, at www.unorc.or.id/ index.php?option=com_content&task=view&id=590&Itemid=236.

———, and R. Sugiarto. 2007. Building back Aceh better through reconstruction and reintegration. Tokyo. August 8. Accessed at November 28, 2010 at isss.org/conferences/.../20070808-isss-1145-mangkusubroto.pdf.

Marston, Richard. 2005. Geography and the Indian Ocean tsunami. *AAG Newsletter* 40(2): 1, 4.

McCulloch, L. 2005. *Aceh: Then and now.* London: Minority Rights Group International.

McDowell, Christopher. 1996. *A Tamil diaspora: Sri Lankan migration, settlement and politics in Switzerland.* Providence, RI: Bergahn Books.

McEwan, Ian. 2005. *Saturday.* Toronto: Alfred A. Knopf (Toronto: Vintage Canada edition 2006).

McGilvray, Dennis. 1982. Mukkuvar Vannimai: Tamil caste and matriclan ideology in Batticaloa. In *Caste, ideology, and interaction,* 34–97. Ed. Dennis McGilvray. Cambridge: Cambridge University Press.

———. 1989. Households in Akkaraipattu: Dowry and domestic organization among matrilineal Tamils and Moors of Sri Lanka. In *Society from the inside out: Anthropological perspectives on the South Asian household,* 192–235. Ed. J.N. Gray and D.J. Mearns. London: Sage.

McGregor, Andrew. 2010. Cyclone Nargis: A case for humanitarian intervention? *Political Geography* 29, 3–4.

Mehrotra, S. 2002. International development targets and official development assistance. *Development and Change* 33(3): 529–38.

Mercer, Claire. 2003. Performing partnership: Civil society and the illusions of good governance in Tanzania. *Political Geography* 22: 741–63.

Mercer, C., G. Mohan, and M. Power. 2004. Towards a critical political geography of African development. *Geoforum* 34(4): 419–36.

Merikallio, K. 2005. The Aceh peace talks. *Suomen Kuvalehti,* February 4.

Miller, M.A. 2006. What's special about special autonomy in Aceh? In *Verandah of violence: The background to the Aceh problem,* 292–314. Ed. A. Reid. Seattle: University of Washington Press.

Mittelman, J.H. 1988. *Out from underdevelopment: Prospects for the third world.* Basingstoke: Macmillan Press.

Modus. 2005. Aktor di balik pertemuan Helsinki. *Modus* 1 (April 18–30): 13.

Mohanty, Chandra Talpade. 2003. Under western eyes: Feminist scholarship and colonial discourse. In *Feminism without borders: Decolonizing theory, practicing solidarity,* 17–42. Durham, NC: Duke University Press.

Mongia, Radhika V. 1999. Race, nationality, mobility: A history of the passport. *Public Culture* 11: 527–56.

MONLAR and ANRHR (Movement for National Land and Agricultural Reform and Alliance for Protection of National Resources and Human Rights). 2005. Tsunami Update II. *Lines* (e-journal) 3(4). Accessed June 2, 2005, at http://www.linesmagazine.org/tsunami/MonlarJan22.htm.

Moore, Mick. 1990. Economic liberalization versus political pluralism in Sri Lanka? *Modern Asian Studies* 24(2): 341–83.

Morokvasic-Müller, M. 2004. From pillars of Yugoslavism to targets of violence: Interethnic marriages in the former Yugoslavia and thereafter. In *Sites of violence: Gender and conflict zones,* 134–51. Ed. W. Giles and J. Hyndman. Berkeley: University of California Press.

MoU (Memorandum of Understanding between the Government of the Republic of Indonesia and the Free Aceh Movement). 2005. Original text, green booklet. August 15.

Mountz, Alison. 2003. Human smuggling, the transnational imaginary and everyday geographies of the nation-state. *Antipode* 35(3): 622–44.

———. 2004. Embodying the nation-state: Canada's response to human smuggling. *Political Geography* 23(3): 323–45.

———. 2007. From protection to securitization: Contemporary geographies of asylum, detention, and activism. Annual Meeting of the Association of American Geographers. San Francisco. April 17–21.

———. 2010. *Seeking asylum: Human smuggling and bureaucracy at the border.* Minneapolis: University of Minnesota Press.

———. Forthcoming. The transnationalization of border enforcement: Refugees, irregular migrants, and the shifting geographies of enforcement. *International Migration Review.*

———, and J. Hyndman. 2006. Feminist approaches to the global intimate. *Women's Studies Quarterly* 34(1–2): 446–63.

Muggah, R. 2008. *Relocation failures in Sri Lanka: A short history of internal displacement and resettlement.* London: Zed Books.

Munro, L.T. 2005. Focus-pocus? Thinking critically about whether aid organizations should do fewer things in fewer countries. *Development and Change* 36(3): 425–47.

Muttiah, M.P. 2005. More women among tsunami dead. *Sunday Observer,* August 14.

Mydans, Seth. 2007. A rebel-turned-governor takes the wheel in Indonesia. *New York Times*, April 14.

Nah, Alice M., and Tim Bunnell. 2005. Ripples of hope: Acehnese refugees in post-tsunami Malaysia. *Singapore Journal of Tropical Geography* 26(2): 249–56.

Nanthikesan, S. 2005. Editorial: Post-tsunami posturing. *Lines* (e-journal) 3(4). (no longer online)

Nelson, Dean. 2005. Old prejudices keep tsunami aid from Tamils. *Sunday Times*, December 18. Accessed July 19, 2008, at http://www.timesonline.co.uk/tol/news/world/article767365.ece.

Nesiah, V., S. Nanthikesan, and A. Kadirgamar. 2005. Post-tsunami reconstruction—new challenges, new directions. *Lines* (e-journal) 3(4). Accessed July 10, 2008, at http://www.lines-magazine.org/tsunami/linestsunamivision.htm.

Nessen, William. 2006. Sentiments made visible: The rise and reason of Aceh's national liberation movement. In *Verandah of violence: The background to the Aceh problem*, 177–198. Ed. A. Reid. Seattle: University of Washington Press.

Neuwirth, T., et al. 2006. *Aceh: Building a sustainable peace—beyond the cessation of hostilities*. Accessed December 11, 2008, at http://www.publicinternationallaw.org/programs/peace/modules/Aceh-Building%20a%20Sustainable%20Peace.pdf.

Newton, M. 2010. The future of the world in Haiti. University of Toronto. January 26. Accessed February 19, 2010, at http://www.news.utoronto.ca/commentary/the-future-of-the-world-in-haiti.html.

New York Times. 2009. Sichuan earthquake. Accessed January 25, 2010, at http://topics.nytimes.com/topics/news/science/topics/earthquakes/sichuan_province_china/index.html

Ò Tuathail, Gearoíd. 2003. "Just out looking for a fight": American affect and the invasion of Iraq. *Antipode* 34: 856–70.

————. 2006. Geopolitical discourses: Paddy Ashdown and the tenth anniversary of the Dayton Peace Accords. *Geopolitics* 11: 141–58.

OCHA (Office for Coordination of Humanitarian Affairs). n.d. Guiding principles on internal displacement. Accessed May 20, 2005, at http://www.reliefweb.int/ocha_ol/pub/idp_gp/idp.html.

OECD (Organization for Economic Cooperation and Development). 1992. Developing countries, meeting of the council at ministerial level. Article 23. May. Accessed July 8, 2008, at www.g7.utoronto.ca/oecd/oecd92.htm.

————. 2002. Development Co-operation Review—Canada. Organization for Economic Cooperation and Development. Paris. Accessed July 8, 2008,

at http://www.oecd.org/document/61/0,2340,en_2649_33721_2409533_
1_1_1_1,00.html.

———. 2005. Paris Declaration on Aid Effectiveness. Accessed July 8, 2008,
at http://www.oecd.org/dataoecd/11/41/34428351.pdf.

OECD-DAC. 2008. The Paris Declaration, DCD-DAC. Accessed July 8, 2008, at
http://www.oecd.org/document/18/0,2340,en_2649_3236398_35401554_
1_1_1_1,00.html.

Olds, Kris, James D. Sidaway, and Matthew Sparke. 2005. Editorial: White
death. *Environment and Planning D: Society and Space* 23: 475–79.

Oxfam International. 2005. The tsunami's impact on women. Oxfam Briefing
Note. March. Accessed December 16, 2006, at http://www.oxfam.org.uk/
what_we_do/issues/conflict_disasters/downloads/bn_tsunami_women
.pdf.

Pain, Rachel. 2009. Globalized fear: Towards an emotional geopolitics. *Progress
in Human Geography* 33: 466–86.

Palmer, B. 2007. The price of peace. *Inside Indonesia* 90. Accessed on November 30, 2007, at http://insideindonesia.org/content/view/124/47/.

Pan, E. 2005. Interview with Sidney Jones on Aceh Peace Agreement. Council
on Foreign Relations. Accessed August 30, 2005, at http://www.cfr.
org/publication/8790/interview_with_sidney_jones_on_aceh_peace_
agreement.html.

Pathoni, Ahmad. 2006. Still shaking, Asia marks tsunami. *Globe and Mail*, December 27.

Perera, Amantha. 2005. The buffer zone fiasco. *Sunday Leader*, December 25.

Perera, Jehan. 2005. NGO attack. *Daily Mirror*, May 9.

Prasodjo, I., and H. Hamid. 2005. *Reconstruction in Aceh*. Washington DC:
Aceh Recovery Forum. May 13.

Pronk, J.P. 2001. Aid as catalyst. *Development and Change* 32(4): 611–29.

Rathgeber, Eva. 1990. WID, WAD, GAD: Trends in Research and Practice.
Journal of Developing Areas 24(4): 489–502.

Rayan, M. 2007. Peace deal helps to rebuild Aceh, but pains remain. *Jakarta Post*,
August 16. Accessed February 22, 2008, at http://www.asia-pacificaction
.org/southeastasia/indonesia/netnews/2007/ind30v11.htm#Peace%20deal
%20helps%20to%20rebuild%20Aceh,%20but%20pains%20remain.

Reid, Anthony. 2006. *Verandah of violence: The background to the Aceh problem*.
Seattle: University of Washington Press.

Renner, Michael. 2006a. Learning from Aceh. *Open Democracy*, January 1. Accessed February 23, 2007, at http://www.opendemocracy.net/conflict-
protest/aceh_3173.jsp.

————. 2006b. Unexpected promise: Disaster creates an opening for peace in a conflict-riven land. *World Watch* 19(6): 10-16. Accessed February 27, 2008, at http://www.worldwatch.org/node/4663.

Reuters. 2010. Office closed in Sri Lanka after protests. *New York Times,* July 8.

Revkin, A.C. 2010. Building safer schools in poor, shaky places. *New York Times,* January 23. Accessed January 25, 2010, at http://dotearth.blogs.nytimes .com/2010/01/23/building-safer-schools-in-poor-shaky-places/?scp= 2&sq=sichuan%20earthquake%202008%20&st=cse.

Ross, M.L. 2003. *Resources and rebellion in Indonesia.* Los Angeles: University of California Press.

Ruwanpura, Kanchana. 2006. Conflict and survival: Sinhala female-headship in eastern Sri Lanka. *Asian Population Studies* 2(2): 187–200.

————, and Jane Humphries. 2004. Mundane heroines: Conflict, ethnicity, gender and female headship in eastern Sri Lanka. *Feminist Economics* 10(2): 173–205.

Ryter, L. 2000. Medan gets a new mayor: A tale of two cities. Part 1. *Inside Indonesia,* 63.

Sallot, J. 2005. Canada discovering foreign aid easier said than done. *Globe and Mail,* June 23.

Sambandan, V.S. 2005. Tsunami and rehabilitation: The rebuilding phase. *Frontline: India's National Magazine from the publishers of The Hindu.* 4(February 22): 12–25.

Schulze, K.E. 2003. The struggle for an independent Aceh: The ideology, capacity, and strategy of GAM. *Studies in Conflict and Terrorism* 26: 241–71.

————. 2004. *The Free Aceh Movement [GAM]: Anatomy of a separatist organization.* Washington DC: East–West Center.

————. 2007. *Mission not so impossible: The Aceh monitoring mission and lessons learned for the EU.* Policy Analysis. Berlin: Friedrich-Ebert-Stiftung.

Seager, Joni. 2006. Editorial: Noticing gender (or not) in disasters. *Geoforum* 37: 2–3.

Sengupta, Somini. 2006. Sri Lanka rebels critic silenced by bullet. *New York Times,* November 26.

Serambi. 2007. BRR will also handle reintegration tasks. April 25.

————. 2008a. Pasca-MoU kejahatan bersenpi meningkat. April 2.

————. 2008b. Hasil survei bank dunia: Investor keluhkan pajak liar di Aceh. May 28.

Shie, T. 2004. Disarming for peace and development in Aceh. *Peace, Conflict and Development* 6.

Shums, Shezna. 2005. Gender discrimination in post-tsunami rebuilding. *Sunday Leader,* August 14.

Sidaway, James D. 2003. Sovereign excesses? Portraying postcolonial sover-
eigntyscapes. *Political Geography* 22: 157–78.

———. 2006. *The colonial present* by D. Gregory, a book review. *Environment
and Planning D: Society and Space* 24: 313–16.

———, Victor R. Savage, and Carl Grundy-Warr. 2008. Editorial: In the tracks
of disaster. In *Singapore Journal of Tropical Geography* 29 (3): 245–250.

Simpson, Edward. 2008. Was there discrimination in the distribution of resources afer the earthquake in Gujarat? Imagination, epistemology, and the
state in western India. Working Paper. London: London School of Economics and Political Science.

Simpson, J. 2006. All politics is global—so get used to it. *Globe and Mail*, October 7.

———. 2010. When it comes to Haiti, things only get worse. *Globe and Mail*,
January 16.

Siriwardene, Regie, K. Indrapala, Sunil Bastian, and S. Kottegoda. 1982. *School
textbooks and communal relations in Sri Lanka*. Part 1. Colombo: Council
for Communal Harmony Through the Media.

Sivanandan, Ambalavaner. 1990. Sri Lanka: A case study. In *Communities
of resistance: Writing on black struggles for socialism*, 199–248. London:
Verso.

Slater, David, and Morag Bell. 2002. Aid and the geopolitics of the post-colonial:
Critical reflections on new Labour's overseas development strategy. *Development and Change* 33(3): 335–60.

Smillie, Ian. 2004. ODA: Options and challenges for Canada. Commissioned
by Canadian Council for International Cooperation. February/March. Accessed July 8, 2008, at http://www.ccic.ca/e/docs/002_policy_2004-
03_oda_options_smillie_report.pdf.

Smith, B. 2009. Ottawa denounces Sri Lankan embassy attack. *Toronto Star*,
May 28.

Smith, Neil. 2006. There is no such thing as "natural" disaster. *Understanding
Katrina: Perspectives From the Social Sciences (SSRC)*, June 11. Accessed February 29, 2008, at http://understandingkatrina.ssrc.org/Smith/.

Sobhan, R. 2002. Aid effectiveness and policy ownership. *Development and
Change* 33(3): 359–48.

Sparke, Matthew B. 2006. A neoliberal nexus: Economy, security, and the
biopolitics of citizenship on the border. *Political Geography* 25(2): 151–80.

———. 2005. *In the Space of Theory: Postfoundational Geographies of the Nation-
State* (Minneapolis: University of Minnesota Press).

Spencer, Jonathan, ed. 1990. *Sri Lanka: History and the roots of conflict*. London:
Routledge.

Sri Lankan Government and Development Partners. 2005. Post-tsunami re-
    covery and construction joint report. December.

Sriskandarajah, D. 2002. The migration-development nexus: Sri Lanka case
    study. Paper prepared for the Centre for Development Research study:
    Migration-Development Links: Evidence and Policy Options. Magdalen
    College, Oxford, United Kingdom.

Statistics Canada. 2001. Immigrant status and period of immigration (10A)
    and place of birth of respondent (260) for immigrants and non-permanent
    residents, for Canada, Provinces, Territories, Census Metropolitan Areas
    and Census.

Stokke, Kristian. 1998. Sinhalese and Tamil nationalism as post-colonial proj-
    ects from above, 1948–1983. *Political Geography* 17(1): 83–113.

————. 2005. After the tsunami: A missed opportunity for peace in Sri Lanka?
    NIASnytt (Nordic Institute of Asian Studies, Asia Insights) (Copenhagen,
    Denmark) 2: 12–20.

————. 2006. Building the Tamil Eelam state: Emerging state institutions and
    forms of governance in LTTE-controlled areas in Sri Lanka. *Third World
    Quarterly* 27(6): 1021–40.

Sukarsono, Achmad. 2005. Tsunami-hit Indonesia to get buffer zone. Reuters
    Foundation, posted on Relief Web. Accessed February 10, 2008, at http://
    www.reliefweb.int/rw/rwb.nsf/db900SID/DDAD69DUXH?Open
    Document.

Sukma, R. 2004. *Security operations in Aceh: Goals, consequences and lessons.* Wash-
    ington DC: East–West Center.

Sulistiyanto, P. 2001 Whither Aceh? *Third World Quarterly* 22(3): 437–52.

Sunday Times. 2006. Coast conservation buffer zone limits relaxed (a RADA
    ad). February 5.

Suud, Y.A. 2005. Reporting at a critical time. *Acehkita* 25, July 25.

Swamy, MRN. 1996. *Tigers of Lanka: From boys to guerillas.* 2nd edition. Co-
    lombo: Vijitha Yapa Bookshop.

Tapol. 2004. Military operations in Aceh fail. *Bulletin Online.* 176.

TEC (Tsunami Evaluation Coalition). 2006. Joint evaluation of the international
    response to the Indian Ocean tsunami: Final report. London: Tsunami Eval-
    uation Coalition.

Tempo. 2005. Martti Ahtisaari: The human rights court in Aceh will not act
    retroactively. *Tempo Magazine,* August 23.

Thiruchelvam, Neelan. 1996. Sri Lanka's ethnic conflict and preventive action:
    The role of NGOs. In *Vigilance and vengeance: NGOs preventing ethnic con-
    flict in divided societies,* 147–64. Ed. R. Rotberg. Washington DC: Brookings
    Institution.

Tissera, Brian. 2005. Buffer zone a hindrance—GL. *Island,* February 19.

UN News Centre. 2010. UN political chief heads to Sri Lanka for talks on reconciliation and rights. Accessed June 18, 2010, at http://www.un.org/apps/news/story.asp?NewsID=35016&Cr=sri+lanka&Cr1=.

UNSG (United Nations Secretary General). 2006. In message to commemoration, secretary-general says major progress achieved since Indonesian government, Free Aceh Movement signed accord. *Unis Vienna.* August 10. Accessed on November 30, 2007, on http://www.unis.unvienna.org/unis/pressrels/2006/sgsm10592.html.

UTHR(J) (University Teachers for Human Rights, Jaffna). 1989. Report No. 1. Accessed July 8, 2008, at http://www.uthr.org/Reports/Report1/Report1.htm.

Uyangoda, Jayadeva. 2005. Ethnic conflict, the Sri Lankan state and the tsunami. *Forced Migration Review.* Special issue (tsunami) no. 24. Accessed August 24, 2005, at www.fmreview.org/pdf/uyangoda.pdf.

Valentine, Gill. 2007. Theorizing and researching intersectionality: A challenge for feminist geography. *Professional Geographer* 59(1): 10–21.

Van Dijk, C. 1981. *Rebellion under the banner of Islam. Darul Islam in Indonesia.* The Hague: Martinus Nijhoff.

Waizenegger, Arno. 2007. Secessionist conflicts and the 2004 Indian Ocean tsunami. *Canada Asia Commentary* 43. Vancouver: Asia Pacific Foundation of Canada.

———, and J. Hyndman. 2010. Two solitudes: Post-tsunami and post-conflict Aceh. *Disasters* 34(3): 787–808.

Walters, William. 2004. Secure borders, safe haven, domopolitics. *Citizenship Studies* 8(3): 237–60.

Wandelt, I. 2005. Indonesiens dreissigjähriger krieg vor seinem ende? *Focus Asien* 12: 14–19.

Ward, O. 2010a. Reflections, forecasts in re-imaging Haiti. *Toronto Star,* January 24.

———. 2010b. In land of graft, can foreign aid find its mark? *Toronto Star,* January 30.

———. 2010c. Is Haiti's Préval buckling under? *Toronto Star,* February 3.

Wayland, Sarah. 2004. Nationalist networks and transnational opportunities: The Sri Lankan Tamil diaspora. *Review of International Studies* 30 (2004): 405–26.

Whatmore, Sarah. 2002. *Hybrid geographies: Natures, cultures, spaces.* London: Sage.

———. 2006. Materialist returns: Practising cultural geography in and for a more-than-human world. *Cultural Geographies* 13: 600–609.

Wisner, B., P. Blaikie, T. Cameron, and I. Davis. 2004. *At Risk.* 2nd edition. London: Routledge. Accessed February 21, 2010, at http://www.unisdr.org/eng/library/ Literature/7235.pdf (1–124).

Women and Media Collective. 2005. One year after the tsunami! (Ad with INFORM and Coalition of Tsunami Affected Women). *Daily Mirror,* December 26.

World Bank. 1998. *Assessing aid: What works, what doesn't and why.* New York: Oxford University Press.

———. 2006a. *Aceh public expenditure analysis: Spending for reconstruction and poverty reduction.* Jakarta: World Bank.

———. 2006b. *GAM reintegration needs assessment: Enhancing peace through community-level development programming.* Jakarta: World Bank.

———. 2007. *2006 village survey in Aceh: An assessment of infrastructure and social conditions by Kecamatan Development Program.* Jakarta: World Bank.

World Bank/DSF. 2007a. *Aceh conflict monitoring update April 2007.* Jakarta: World Bank/DSF.

———. 2007b. *Aceh conflict monitoring update December 2007.* Jakarta: World Bank/DSF.

———. 2008a. *Aceh conflict monitoring update April 2008.* Jakarta: World Bank/DSF.

———. 2008b. *Aceh conflict monitoring update May/June 2008.* Jakarta: World Bank/DSF.

Yudhoyono, Susilo Bambang. 2006. Keynote speech at the opening of the international conference, Building permanent peace in Aceh: One year after the Helsinki Accord. August 14. Accessed July 9, 2010, at http://www.indonesia-ottawa.org/information/details.php?type=speech&id=89.

Yuval-Davis, N. 1998. *Gender and nation.* London: Sage.

Zeccola, P. Forthcoming. Dividing disasters in Aceh, Indonesia: Separatist conflict and tsunami, human rights and humanitarianism. *Disasters.*

Interviews and Personal Communication

Aceh

Interview #17: Activist working for a local NGO, Banda Aceh, May 21, 2006.
Interview #25: GAM ex-combatant, Aceh Timur, June 25, 2006.
Interview #37: Academic and peace talks observer, Singapore, June 1, 2006.
Interview #101: Former AMM delegate, Sabang, April 3, 2007.
Interview #115: Field worker for a local NGO, Pidie, May 3, 2007.

Interview #201: Former GAM commander, now KPA and BRR, Banda Aceh, June 2, 2007.

Interview #202: Lawyer at a local NGO, Banda Aceh, June 2, 2007.

Interview #205: Livelihoods trainer, Banda Aceh, June 3, 2007.

Interview #208: Former prisoner of war, returned refugee from Europe, Pidie, June 4, 2007.

Interview #213: Head of new political party, former student activist, Banda Aceh, June 5, 2007.

Interview #308: Local woman activist working for the BRR, Banda Aceh, May 31, 2008.

Interview #320: Local ex-contractor, now working for an INGO, Banda Aceh, June 5, 2008.

Interview #322: Reintegration adviser for an INGO, Banda Aceh, June 6, 2008.

Interview #328: Program manager of an INGO, Banda Aceh, June 20, 2008.

Interview #330: INGO country manager, Banda Aceh, June 14, 2008.

Interview #333: Activist working for a peace-mediating INGO, Aceh Timur, June 21, 2008.

Interview #340: Humanitarian activist working for a local NGO, Lhokseumawe, June 25, 2008.

Canada

Interview #12: Two senior managers, CIDA, Hull, Quebec, June 12, 2002.

Interview #13: Senior manager, CIDA, Hull, Quebec, June 13, 2002.

Interview #35: Senior manager, CIDA, Hull, Quebec, July 25, 2005.

Interview #36: CIDA manager, Hull, Quebec, July 26, 2005.

Personal communication: Former Canadian civil servant, October 1, 2004.

Sri Lanka

Interview #2: CIDA representative, Colombo, July 12, 2002.

Interview #9: Senior managers, CIDA Programme Support Unit, Colombo, February 9, 2005.

Interview #17: Canadian diplomat, Colombo, July 17, 2002.

Interview #18: Canadian high commissioner to Sri Lanka, Colombo, July 18, 2002.

Interview #25: Canadian high commissioner to Sri Lanka, Colombo, February 25, 2005.

Interview #29: Senior managers, CIDA Programme Support Unit, February 9, 2005.

Interview #103: International aid official, conducted by Soundarie David, Colombo, June 8, 2007.

Interview #105: International aid official, conducted by Soundarie David, Colombo, June 10, 2007.

Index

About the Author

Jennifer Hyndman is Professor at the Centre for Refugee Studies at York University in Toronto, Canada. Her research spans the continuum of forced migration, from conflict zones to refugee camps and resettlement in North America. Her work problematizes taken for granted understandings of displacement, security, and geopolitics of asylum. She is the author of the book *Managing Displacement: Refugees and the Politics of Humanitarianism* (University of Minnesota Press, 2000) and co-editor of and contributor to *Sites of Violence: Gender and Conflict Zones* (University of California Press, 2004).

Also from Kumarian Press...

Humanitarianism:

How the Aid Industry Works: An Introduction to International Development
Arjan de Haan

Development and Humanitarianism: Practical Issues
Edited by Deborah Eade and Tony Vaux

Humanitarianism Under Fire:
The US and UN Intervention in Somalia
Kenneth Rutherford

Humanitarian Crises and Intervention:
Reassessing the Impact of Mass Media
Walter Soderlund, E. Donald Briggs, Kai Hildebrandt,
and Abdel Salam Sidahmed

New and Forthcoming:

Class Dynamics of Agrarian Change
Henry Bernstein

The Struggle for Civil Society in Central Asia:
Crisis and Transformation
Charles Buxton

Inside the Everyday Lives of Development Workers:
The Challenges and Futures of Aidland
Edited by Anne-Meike Fechter and Heather Hindman

Women and War: Gender Identity and Activism in Times of Conflict
Joyce Kaufman and Kristen Williams

Visit Kumarian Press at **www.kpbooks.com** or call **toll-free**
800.232.0223 for a complete catalog.

Kumarian Press, located in Sterling, Virginia, is a forward-looking, scholarly press that promotes active international engagement and an awareness of global connectedness.